Museums of Boston

Westholme Museum Guides

Museums of Atlanta

Museums of Boston

Museums of Chicago

Museums of Los Angeles

Museums of New York City

Museums of Philadelphia

Museums of San Francisco

Museums of Washington, DC

Visiting museums is one of the best ways to get to know a city. Westholme Museum Guides, designed for both residents and visitors, are the first-ever uniform compilations of permanent collections open to the public in America's major cities. Each city has its own unique group of museums, some famous, others practically unknown, but all of them are important parts of our nation's cultural life.

Museums of Boston

A Guide for Residents and Visitors

Nicole Berard

WESTHOLME
Yardley

Acknowledgments
Many thanks to the various museum and National Park Service staff who have made this book possible. You do a great public service by maintaining these collections. Thanks also to Christine Liddie for the exceptional copyediting work and John Hubbard for the fantastic cover design. And special thanks to my family, friends, and Scott Hovey, who is a little of both.

Published by Westholme Publishing, LLC, Eight Harvey Avenue, Yardley, Pennsylvania 19067.

Maps by Joseph John Clark

10 9 8 7 6 5 4 3 2 1
First Printing

ISBN: 978-159416-047-9

ISBN 10: 1-59416-047-3

Visit our Web site: www.westholmepublishing.com

Printed in the United States of America on acid-free paper.

For my mom,

SUSAN BERARD-GOLDBERG,

who loves a good collection.

Contents

Introduction

In 1630, John Winthrop led a group of Puritan colonists from England to a peninsula on Massachusetts Bay known to Native Americans as Shawmut. Dissatisfied with their nearby Salem colony, the Puritans decided to make Shawmut their permanent home and renamed it Boston after the British city from which they'd departed. The new city was incorporated on November 17, 1630.

Even before there was a United States of America, the city of Boston, Massachusetts, had begun to establish itself as an intellectual and cultural center. As colonial dissent brewed alongside Sam Adam's beer, seventeenth-century Boston attracted more than its share of theologians, philosophers, and writers. Academic institutions sprang up around these great minds, and the city began its tenure as America's university town. (In fact, Harvard University was founded in 1636, just six years after Boston was settled.)

In addition, Boston's geographic location made it the New World's closest port to Europe. Following the American Revolution of 1776, the city became one of the wealthiest trading ports in the world, exporting timber, tobacco, rum, and fish. Likewise, goods from around the world flooded the young city, and Bostonians developed a reputation for cultural elitism. By the nineteenth century, the city was known as a center for the arts.

It is from this combination of academic tradition and favorable trade conditions that many of Boston's modern museums evolved. Another decisive factor was the 1791 arrival of Philadelphian Daniel Bowen, a close friend of artist and museum advocate Charles Willson Peale. Bowen made his way to Boston with a small collection of waxworks and English paintings, intent on opening a great museum. After mounting modest exhibits in coffee houses and schools, Bowen's museum established permanent residence on Tremont Street, and was rechristened the Columbia Museum in 1801.

Bowen's exhibits included fine art by romantic painter Washington Allston, telegraph inventor Samuel F. B. Morse, and miniaturist Edward Greene Malbone. On a more low-brow note, the museum showcased lavish waxworks and an alcoholic elephant reputed to drink 30 bottles of porter a day. At the time, museum keeping was a for-profit venture, and culture was laced through with common spectacle in an effort to lure visitors. Bowen did well. Although a series of fires destroyed two early locations, the museum persevered and had a significant influence on the Boston landscape until it merged with the rival New England Museum of Natural History.

The New England Museum of Natural History had its start in 1814, when a group of doctors and scientists gathered to form the Linnaean Society and preserve their artifacts in a suitable museum. By 1874, the museum was housed in Boston's Back Bay, in what is now Louis of Boston. Following the

World Wars, the museum reopened in a new location as The Museum of Science, as it remains to this day.

During the eighteenth and nineteenth centuries, several elite Bostonians amassed personal collections that they later donated to the city. First and foremost was Isabella Stewart Gardner's fine-art collection, much of which was purchased on exotic expeditions around the globe. "Isabella of Boston," as the papers called the socialite, planned much of the museum herself, on a personal mission to bring art to the people. Other privileged households were turned into museums following the owner's demise, as was the case for the Charles Hammond Gibson House and the Otis House Museum. In still other instances, the site of an historic event has been enriched by a family's collection. For example, the Longfellow House and Adams National Historical Park display artifacts, including impressive libraries, from multiple generations of family.

Of course, few events affected Boston history as much as the American Revolution, which began just outside the city in Concord, MA. Visitors can follow the events leading up to the "shot heard 'round the world" at institutions such as Paul Revere's House, the Concord Museum, and the Museum of our National Heritage in Lexington. Arlington's George A. Smith Museum features authentic Revolutionary War bullet holes at the site where British soldiers bayoneted a local man to death. The Museum of the Ancient and Honorable Artillery Company and the USS Constitution Museum also pay tribute to our military history.

The fine tradition of national history museums continues in Boston today, with twentieth-century attractions like the John

F. Kennedy Library and Museum. Kennedy's library pays much attention to the Civil Rights movement, but Boston was on the forefront of African American rights long before the murdered president. The Afro-American History Museum caps Boston's Black Freedom Trail and resides at the site of the country's first schoolhouse for African American students. The Museum of the National Center for Afro-American Artists features work by Black artists all over the world, concentrating on local talent. Visitors will also find museums dedicated to the Armenian, Jewish, and French populations of this diverse city.

As mentioned, Boston's array of colleges and universities has played a huge role in the city's museums. Boston University, Boston College, Harvard, Tufts, MIT, and Brandeis all open their collections for public viewing at little or no cost. Not only will you find treasures by internationally known artists, you'll see work by tomorrow's masters before the rest of the world does. And scientifically speaking, who is a better authority than MIT or Harvard Med? From holograms to hollow skulls, these institutions are the last word in scientific art and artifact.

Naturally, not every Boston attraction counts as a museum. In addition to the collections described in this book, Boston features a great number of attractions worth a visit. Boston Common and the Public Gardens, in the center of the Back Bay neighborhood, are a must for any tourist. In the summer, hitch a ride on the unique Public Garden Swan Boats for a quintessential Boston experience. Nearby, the winding cobbled streets of Beacon Hill are a convincing substitute for Europe, complete with boutiques and cafés. Animal lovers will appreciate the Franklin Park Zoo, the New England Aquarium, and the variety of whale-watch tours departing Boston Harbor (whose islands make for a fun summer outing). As a world-class city, Boston hosts thousands of cultural events yearly in its theaters, clubs, and arenas. For current listings, visitors should consult the local papers—*The Boston Globe*, *The Boston Herald*, *The Weekly Dig*, and *The Boston Phoenix*—or the corresponding Web sites.

Boston has always been a city of neighborhoods, each with its own characteristic culture. Within city limits, visitors will notice the differences between North End and South End, Dorchester and Jamaica Plain, Allston-Brighton and Boston proper. Towns immediately outside the city are considered part of the Greater Boston area, including Brookline, Cambridge, Somerville, Newton, and Quincy. For this book, I've chosen to include institutions in all of these towns, as well as a few important listings further outside the region, such as the Salem Witchcraft Museum and the Peabody Essex. I've used MBTA service as a rough guideline. With a few noted exceptions, destinations in this volume are public-transportation accessible. There are also numerous city tours that cover some museums; ask the visitor's center or hotel concierge for brochures.

Those who plan to spend a more substantial amount of time in Boston might consider renting a car and venturing outside the city. Less than an hour away, the city of Worcester, MA, features both the dignified Worcester Art Museum and the somewhat less delicate American Sanitary Plumbing Museum. Springfield, in central Massachusetts, is home to the Naismith Memorial Basketball Hall of Fame, the Indian Motorcycle Museum Hall, the Springfield Armory Museum, and The Springfield Museums of Science, Art, and History. In the western corner of the state, North Adams hosts the stunning Massachusetts Museum of Contemporary Art (MassMOCA) in a converted factory. For such a small geographic area, Massachusetts packs a serious cultural wallop.

Using *Museums of Boston*

For the purposes of this book, a museum is defined as a permanent collection of primarily nonreproduction artifacts. I've made a few exceptions for especially important galleries and university museums that do not have large permanent collections, as these institutions have a potent cultural impact on the community. Contemporary art fans should make time to visit Boston's many small galleries and open studios, which are listed in regional papers.

Each entry in this volume includes the museum's formal name (an index of alternative names can be found in the appendix), address, phone number, and Web site, as well as hours, admission costs, and directions.

I have tried to keep each entry neutral, as personal taste varies, and what one woman finds fascinating, another might find to be a terrible bore. I've included museum highlights in some entries, which indicates particularly famous items or collections rather than subjective favorites. I've also compiled lists of museums by subject matter, audience age, and more to help you decide what best suits you and your traveling companions.

Further Reading and Resources

Allison, Robert J. *A Short History of Boston*. Massachusetts: Commonwealth Editions, 2004.

Kennedy, Lawrence W. *Planning the City Upon a Hill*. Massachusetts: University of Massachusetts Press, 1994.

McNulty, Elizabeth. *Boston Then and Now*. California: Thunder Bay Press, 2002.

Visitor Information

For general information about Boston, consult the Massachusetts Office of Travel and tourism before your trip. Their excellent Web site will help you locate lodging, dining, and activities in the Greater Boston Area.

Massachusetts Office of Travel and Tourism
10 Park Plaza, Suite 4510
Boston, MA 02116
617-973-8500; (toll-free) 800-227-MASS (U.S. & Canada)
www.mass-vacation.com

The official Web site of the city of Boston, www.cityof-boston.gov, offers a similar array of features that will guide you to local attractions, tours, and businesses.

Once in Boston, stop by the closest Visitor Information Center for guidance and reading material. Centers are conveniently located in major tourist areas and offer tickets for popular bus and trolley tours. Many centers also have restrooms and vending machines for on-the-go refreshment.

Greater Boston Convention and Visitors Bureau
Two Copley Place, Suite 105
Boston, MA 02116
888-SEE-BOSTON
www.bostonusa.com

Boston Common Visitor Information Center
147 Tremont Street
Boston, MA 02116
617-536-4100

Boston Harbor Islands Information Booth
Long Wharf
Boston, MA 02110
617-223-8666

Boston National Historical Park Visitor Center
15 State Street
Boston, MA 02109
617-242-5642

Charlestown Navy Yard Visitor Center
55 Constitution Rd.
Charlestown, MA 02129
617-242-5601

Regional Transportation

In most cases I've given directions via MBTA (Mass Bay
Transit Authority) public transportation. The "T," as locals call
it, consists of four subway/trolley lines denoted by color, a
regional commuter rail, and hundreds of buses. It's the oldest

mass-transit system in the country, and while it sometime shows its age, it is generally the most inexpensive and efficient way to get around. Best of all, www.mbta.com features a great trip planner, which will help you navigate anywhere the T travels. In a city where parking is scarce and expensive, this is the way to go.

Maps

Each museum in this book is marked on the following maps by its page number. These maps are designed to show the reader the general proximity of the museums to one another.

Museums of Boston

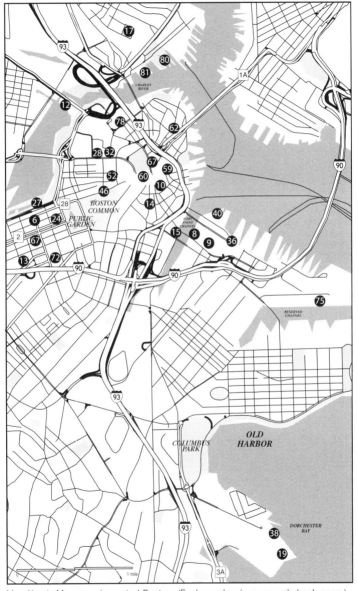

Map No. 1. Museums in central Boston. (Each number is museum's book page.)

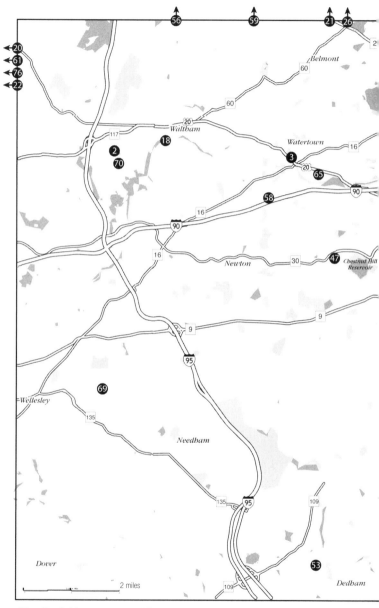

Map No. 2. Museums around Boston. (Each number is museum's book page.)

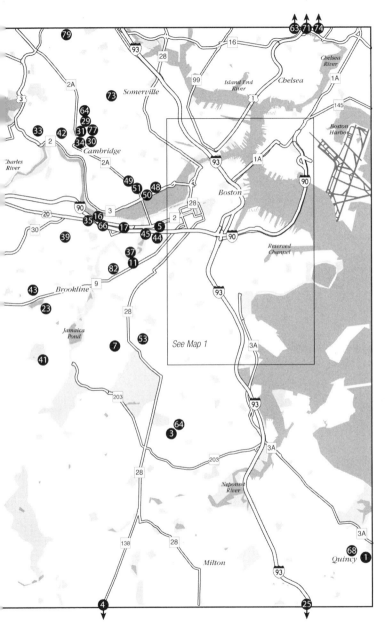

Visual Codes

Architecturally significant

Best to provide own transportation

Exhibits suitable for children

Food available on premises

Must call ahead

Notable art

Notable grounds or garden

Science oriented

Site of historic event

Adams National Historical Park

135 Adams Street
Quincy, MA 02169
617-770-1175
www.nps.gov/adam

Open: Daily, 9:00 AM–5:00 PM (Apr 19–Nov 10); Closed Nov 11–Apr 18.

Admission: Adults, $5.00; Children under 16, Free

Directions: MBTA Red Line train to the Quincy Center Station. Turn right upon exiting the train and at the top of the stairs, turn left and exit the station to Hancock Street. Start your visit at The National Park Service Visitor Center at 1250 Hancock Street.

The Adams National Historical Park is home to the two oldest presidential birthplaces in the United States. Both John Adams (president from 1797 to 1801) and his son John Quincy Adams (president from 1825 to 1829) were born on this property in neighboring houses. The park includes eleven buildings in all, including the birthplaces, the Old House (the Adams family mansion, built in 1730) and the Stone Library. The park museum collections are displayed mainly in the Old House and consist of period furniture, rare books, decorative objects, and historical documents. These objects are almost entirely authentic, supplemented with reproduction wallpaper and upholstery. Provenance aside, many of these artifacts enjoy great intrinsic value, from Queen Anne furniture to seventeenth-century Primitive American paintings. The Stone Library, built to house the Adams' family book collection, holds 12,000 volumes. Notable works include John Adams' copy of George Washington's farewell address and a Bible concordance from 1521.

American Jewish Historical Society–Boston

160 Herrick Road
Newton, MA 02459
617-559-8880
www.ajhsboston.org

Open: M–Th, 9:00 AM–4:00 PM; F, 9:00 AM–12:30 PM
Admission: Free
Directions: MBTA Green D Line to Riverside. As you exit the train, take
the path that continues in the outbound direction to Herrick Road, turn
left onto Herrick and walk up the hill to the campus—a ten- to fifteen-
minute walk.

At its headquarters at Hebrew College, the Boston branch of
the American Jewish Historical Society hosts traveling exhibits
created by the national chapter, as well as smaller displays from
its own collection. The society is the archival repository for the
documentary record of Jewish life in the greater Boston area
and the home of the reference library of the Jewish
Genealogical Society of Greater Boston. Look for exhibits
drawn from this extensive collection of records, photographs,
and personal papers. Recent traveling exhibits have displayed
rare books, artifacts, and even such personal heirlooms as family
circumcision kits. Check the Web site or call to see what's cur-
rently on display.

Armenian Library and Museum of America

65 Main Street
Watertown, MA 02472
617-926-2562
www.almainc.org/

Open: Th, 6:00 PM–9:00 PM; F and Su, 1:00 PM–5:00 PM; Sa, 10:00
AM–2:00 PM; Check Web site for holiday closings.
Admission: Adults, $5.00; Students, $2.00; Members and Children
under 12, Free; Call for holiday closings.
Directions: MBTA #57 bus to Watertown Square

ALMA's staff of more than 100 volunteers lovingly maintains
the largest collection of Armenian cultural items in the United
States. At any given time, at least 400 of the tens of thousands
of items are on display in beautifully curated exhibits that tell
the stories of an ancient and complex culture. Religious artifacts, inscribed rugs, folk costumes, metalwork, paintings,
embroideries, currency, illuminated manuscripts, ceramics,
home furnishings, photographs, musical instruments, and more
find a home in the museum's collection. But the most moving
display is the permanent memorial to the Armenian Genocide
of World War I. It's a powerful exhibit that both terrifies and
inspires with tales of a courageous and determined people.
ALMA's Mesrop Boyajian Library is an invaluable resource
that includes 800 oral histories recorded by genocide survivors.
An ongoing cataloging project means the library's thousands of
volumes will soon be available online.

Blue Hills Trailside Museum

1904 Canton Avenue
Milton, MA 02186
617-333-0690
www.massaudubon.org/bluehills

Open: W–Su and M holidays, 10:00 AM–5:00 PM; Trails open from
dawn until dusk.
Admission: Adults, $3.00; Seniors, $2.00; Children 3–12, $1.50;
Members, Free
Directions: Not MBTA accessible. Take I-93 to exit 2B (Milton, Route
138 North). Go straight through the first set of lights; the museum is
one-half mile ahead on the right.

The 7,000-acre Blue Hills Reservation, managed by the
Massachusetts Audubon Society, is a quick drive from Boston
in scenic Milton. A wonderful spot for hiking and wildlife
viewing, the reservation features an interpretive center—the
Blue Hills Trailside Museum. Inside, the museum exhibits
recreate the natural habitats of local animals, sometimes with
live animals included. Owls, otters, foxes, snakes, and opossums
are just a few of the creatures that make their homes in the
wooded Blue Hills, and children will especially enjoy feeding
the ducks and turkeys at the museum entrance. Native
American artifacts are also on display, and they give a nice historical perspective to any hike. Finish your visit by climbing the
reservation lookout tower and taking in the landscape.

Boston Architectural College

320 Newbury Street
Boston, MA 02155
617-262-5000
www.the-bac.edu/

Open: M–Th, 8:30 AM–10:30 PM; F, 8:30 AM–9:00 PM; Sa, 9:00
AM–5:00 PM; Su, Noon–7:00 PM
Admission: Free
Directions: MBTA green line B, C, or D to Hynes Convention Center

Founded in the 1880s as a club for local architects, the Boston
Architectural College (BAC) is an independent college located
in Boston's Back Bay. BAC offers bachelor's and master's
degrees in architecture and interior design, as well as individual
lectures on architecture, design, real estate, and city planning.
However, the biggest draw for those not seeking higher education are the BAC's two exhibition galleries. Located on the
ground floor, the McCormick Gallery looks out onto a busy
corner of Newbury Street. Its exhibits celebrate the design
process, often featuring work by students and emerging architects. The Stankowicz Gallery, located on the fourth floor, features work by visual artists with a special emphasis on photography and computer-related art.

Boston Athenaeum

10 1/2 Beacon Street
Boston, MA 02108
617-227-0270
www.bostonathenaeum.org

Open: M–F, 9:00 AM–5:00 PM (gallery open until 8:00 PM on M); Sa,
9:00 AM–4:00 PM; Tours Tu and Th, 3:00 PM.
Admission: Free
Directions: MBTA red or green line trains to Park Street Station. Walk
up Park Street toward the State House then take a right onto Beacon
Street.

The Boston Athenaeum, one of the oldest and most distin-
guished independent libraries in the United States, was founded in 1807 by members of the Anthology Society, a group of
scholars led by Ralph Waldo Emerson's father. In 1849, the
Athenaeum moved to its current location at 10 1/2 Beacon
Street, an imposing space modeled after Palladio's Palazzo da
Porta Festa in Vicenza, Italy. While the Athenaeum's heralded
half-million-volume library is available to members only (there
are 1,049 available memberships, many passed from generation
to generation), the building's first art gallery floor is open to
the public. Here, rotating exhibits mix with art and antiquities
from the Athenaeum's private holdings, as well as rare books.
The children's reading room is also open to the public and features secluded nooks for storytime. The rest of the Athenaeum
can be viewed during guided tours twice a week. It is recommended you call ahead to reserve space.

Highlights:

The fifth-floor reading room

Rare books, including George Washington's private library

Paintings by itinerant artist Cephas Thompson

Boston Beer Museum

30 Germania Street
Jamaica Plain, MA 02130
617-522-9080
www.samueladams.com/contact_tour.aspx
Open: Tours Th, 2:00 PM; F, 2:00 PM and 5:50 PM; Sa, Noon, 1:00 PM, and 2:00 PM
Admission: Suggested $2.00 donation to charity
Directions: MBTA Orange line to Stony Brook

It may not be a typical museum, but the Boston Beer Museum at Sam Adams Brewery is a nifty look at the science and history of America's favorite beverage. Sam Adams began brewing at this site in 1984, kicking off the craft-brew movement with its Boston Lager. And even though the main brewery has since moved to a new site, the giant machinery at the Beer Museum brews each Sam Adams flavor at least once annually. You can enjoy a brewmaster-guided tour of this equipment, as well as the science behind the process, and then top it off with a taste of the goods. There is a gift shop on-site to fulfill all your barware needs.

Highlights:

Complimentary product samples

Boston Children's Museum

300 Congress Street
Boston, MA 02210
617-426-6500
www.bostonchildrensmuseum.org

Open: M–Sa, 10:00 AM–5:00 PM; Su, 10:00 AM–9:00 PM. Special holiday hours: Christmas Eve (12/24), 10:00 AM–3:00 PM, and New Year's Eve (12/31), 10:00 AM–3:00 PM; Closed Thanksgiving and Christmas.

Admission: Adults, $9.00; Senior Citizens, $7.00; Children 2–15, $7.00; Children 1–2, $2.00; Children under 1, Free. Target Fridays, $1.00 all visitors from 5:00 PM–9:00 PM

Directions: MBTA red line to South Station. Exit South Station onto Summer Street. Take a right on Summer Street and walk one block toward the water. Turn left onto Dorchester Avenue. At the stoplight, turn right onto Congress Street and cross to the open sidewalk and proceed across the bridge. You'll see the museum ahead on your left, behind the forty-foot milk bottle.

Founded in 1913, The Boston Children's Museum pioneered the kind of "hands-on" learning we now take for granted in most children's museums. From the start, the museum focused on early childhood development through a trio of themes: art, culture, and science. Exhibits designed and built by the museum have traveled around the world, and for good reason. It would be difficult to find a better place for kids to explore and learn. From the first glance of the giant milk bottle outside (home to an ice-cream stand), the Children's Museum is full of magic. Pint-sized visitors can investigate an authentic Japanese house shipped from Kyoto, ring up purchases and learn about nutrition in the "Supermercado" exhibit, and experiment in the Science Playground. Adults will also be entertained by the museum's collection of 50,000+ artifacts. The museum Web site has information on special programs, as well as tips on how parents can make the most of their child's visit.

Highlights:

Grandparent's Attic (dress up in period costumes)

The Recycle Shop (purchase recycled craft material by the bag)

Hall of Toys

Native American wigwam

Boston Fire Museum

344 Congress Street
Boston, MA 02210
617-482-1344
www.bostonfiremuseum.org

Open: Apr–Oct, Th, 11:00 AM–4:00 PM; F, 11:00 AM–9:00 PM, Sa,
11:00 AM–3:00 PM
Admission: Free
Directions: MBTA red line to South Station. Exit South Station onto
Summer Street. Take a right on Summer Street and walk one block
toward the water. Turn left onto Dorchester Avenue. At the stoplight,
turn right onto Congress Street and cross to the open sidewalk and
proceed across the bridge. The Fire Museum is just beyond the Boston
Children's Museum.

In 1938, a group of fire service buffs formed the Boston Sparks
Association to share their enthusiasm and provide canteen
service for local firefighters. Their collection of fire memorabilia was displayed in the South End until the late sixties, when,
ironically, much of it was destroyed in a massive blaze. By 1983,
however, the association had joined forces with an earlier ver-
sion of the Boston Fire Museum and moved into the current
space on Congress Street (now listed on the National Historic
Register). The Boston Fire Museum hosts a beautiful collection of antique firefighting apparatus, as well as fire alarms,
photographs, and related memorabilia. The building itself is a
decommissioned firehouse built in 1891, formerly home to
Engine Companies 38 & 39, and later, Engine 39 and Ladder
18. The Boston Sparks Association has meticulously restored
the station, preserving the strong history of Boston fire service.

Highlights:

A hand-operated Ephraim Thayer pump from 1793

Specialized firefighting tools

Protective gear from modern firefighters

Boston Historical Society and Museum

206 Washington Street
Boston, MA 02109
617-720-1713
www.bostonhistory.org/

Open: Daily, 9:00 AM–5:00 PM. Extended hours in summer. Closed
New Year's Day, Thanksgiving Day, and Christmas.
Admission: Adults, $5.00; Seniors (62 and up) and Students, $4.00;
Children 6–18, $1.00
Directions: MBTA Orange or Blue line to State Street. The museum is
directly upstairs.

The Bostonian Society's museum and library meticulously preserve Boston history from its earliest inhabitants to modern
day. The museum holds roughly 6,500 artifacts and objets d'art,
from maritime relics to fine oil paintings. Each was chosen to
represent the rich culture and history of the city, and displays
are constructed to illustrate the diverse ethnic, socioeconomic,
and political groups that have called Boston home. For an
additional fee, researchers can use the adjoining society library,
which houses thousands of books, photographs, sketches,
maps, and manuscripts. The photo collection is especially vast
and features the Robert B. Severy collection of 6,000 local
streetscapes. Many shots can be found in the museum's online
catalog as well, and reprints are available for a fee.

Boston Museum of Fine Arts

Avenue of the Arts
465 Huntington Avenue
Boston, MA 02115
617-267-9300
TTY: 617-267-9703
www.mfa.org/

Open: M–Tu, 10:00 AM–4:45 PM; W–F, 10:00 AM–9:45 PM; Sa–Su,
10:00 AM–4:45 PM; Check Web site for special exhibit hours.
Admission: Adults, $15.00; Seniors and Students, $13.00; Children
7–17, $6.50; Children 6 and under and Museum Members, Free
Directions: MBTA green line E to Museum of Fine Arts

Established in 1870, the Museum of Fine Arts (commonly
called the MFA) is the mother of all Boston art museums.
Over a million people take in the MFA's extensive collections
every year, and nearly a quarter of them take advantage of lectures, films, performances, and other educational activities
sponsored by the museum. The 400,000 objects in the MFA's
vast collection cover eight curatorial categories: Art of the
Americas; Art of Europe; Art of Asia, Oceania, and Africa;
Art of the Ancient World; Contemporary Art; Prints,
Drawing, and Photographs; Textile and Fashion Art; and
Musical Instruments. There is art to please every taste, a dazzling array that would take many days to fully explore. Fortify
yourself with a snack at one of two cafés or Bravo, the museum's signature restaurant. Or make that a drink when, on the
first Friday of each month, MFA First Fridays turn the museum into a hip cocktail spot. Then grab a map and decide what
you absolutely can't miss.

Highlights:

Museum courtyards and Japanese garden

The Buddhist Temple Room

Egyptian Funerary Arts

American Art

Boston Museum of Science

Science Park
Boston, MA 02114
617-723-2500
www.mos.org

Open: Su–Th and Sa, 9:00 AM–5:00 PM; F, 9:00 AM–9:00 PM; Day
before Thanksgiving and Christmas Eve, 9:00 AM–2:00 PM; Closed
Thanksgiving and Christmas.
Admission: Adults, $16.00; Children, $13.00; Senior Citizens, $14.00.
Special exhibits, Omni Theater, Planetarium, Butterfly Garden, 3D
Theater, and Laser Shows are priced separately. Student discounts are
available with valid ID.
Directions: MBTA Green D Line to Science Park station. The museum is
diagonally across the street.

It's the granddaddy of east-coast science museums, and the
Boston Museum of Science has earned every bit of recognition
it gets. A vast and constantly growing facility, the MoS was
founded in the nineteenth century in Boston's Back Bay in a
handsome building that now houses Louis of Boston, upscale
clothiers. The current location features two wings of exhibits,
the Mugar Omni Theater, the Charles Hayden Planetarium,
and the 3-D Digital Wright Theater. There is not a better
place in the city to learn, experiment, and witness the changing
environments and technology around us. The museum contains
much more than you can possibly see in a day, but a peek at the
MoS Web site will help you figure out an itinerary. From classic exhibits on space, electricity, and dinosaurs to modern
examinations of complex systems, energy, and the human body,
the permanent museum collections are sure to satisfy. The cur-

rent Science and Technology Center showcases the latest happenings in the tech world, and Cahners ComputerPlace and the Discovery Center allow for hands-on exploration. Complete your experience with stargazing atop the museum roof; call the Gilliland Observatory Hotline (617-589-0267) for nightly updates.

Highlights:

Theater of Electricity

Discovery Center

Live presentations—see schedules for planetarium and theaters

Boston Public Library

700 Boylston Street (Copley Square)
Boston, MA 02116
617-536-5400
www.bpl.org

Open: M–Th, 9:00 AM–9:00 PM; F–Sa, 9:00 AM–5:00 PM; Su, 1:00
PM–5:00 PM (Oct–May)
Admission: Free
Directions: MBTA green line to Copley Square. The library is right out-
side of the station.

The central location of the Boston Public Library flanks the
city's famous Copley Square, facing the Trinity Church and
John Hancock Tower across the street. As the first public
municipal library in the United States, it has amassed a collection that goes well beyond its six million circulating books. In
fact, some of the finest art in Boston is on display here, for
free. The perfectly proportioned classical façade of the McKim
building, which houses the BPL research library, hides a series
of ornate galleries with a private courtyard in the center. In
addition to dazzling marble work created specifically for the
library, you will see painting, sculpture, and decorative arts. The
Puvis de Chavannes Gallery, with its mural of the muses, particularly impresses many visitors. From here, you can enter the
Abbey Room, which is dominated by Edwin Austin Abbey's
"The Quest of the Holy Grail." The Sargent and Wiggins
Galleries showcase American painting and prints, respectively.
The library courtyard is one of the best-kept secrets in
Boston's Back Bay: a charming oasis in bustling Copley
Square. In good weather, purchase lunch from Sebastian's Map

Room Café within the library and picnic. You can also reserve a table at Novel, the library's restaurant overlooking the courtyard. Be sure to check the BPL Web site for information on guided tours, rare-book collections, and special presentations. The BPL also maintains a catalog of the library's collection for public use, with information regarding medium, size, date, artist, donor, and more.

Highlights:

Sargent's *Triumph of Religion*

The Wiggins print collection

Boston Stock Exchange

110 Franklin Street
Boston, MA 02110
617-235-2058
www.bostonstock.com

Open: By appointment only. It is recommended that visitors call at least two weeks in advance to reserve space.

Admission: Free

Directions: The Stock Exchange is within walking distance of four MBTA stations. MBTA Orange line to State Street: Exit the station and turn right onto Devonshire Street. Boston Stock Exchange is three blocks down on the right. MBTA Orange or Red line to Downtown Crossing: Exit the station and turn right onto Franklin Street. Boston Stock Exchange is two blocks down on the left. MBTA Red or Green line to Park Street: Exit the station and cross over Tremont Street to Winter Street. Winter Street becomes Summer Street. Travel two blocks and turn left onto Arch Street. Boston Stock Exchange is one block down on the right. MBTA Green line to Government Center: Exit the station and proceed down the steps, turning right onto Congress Street. Congress Street crosses over State Street. Bear right onto Devonshire Street. Boston Stock Exchange is three blocks down on the right.

The Boston Stock Exchange, founded in 1834, is the third-largest stock exchange in the United States. The glass-enclosed viewing area above the trading floor offers a glimpse at the day-to-day operations of this bustling enterprise. Exhibits and multimedia displays trace the close links between the exchange's role as an early source of capital, the development of New England's economy, and the growth of Boston's financial services industry. Guided tours are limited to twenty visitors each and fill up quickly, so be sure to call ahead. Special tours for classrooms can also be arranged in advance.

Boston Tea Party Ship and Museum

380 Dorchester Avenue
Boston, MA 02127
617-338-1773
www.bostonteapartyship.com

Open: The museum is closed for renovations through spring 2008.
Admission: TBA
Directions: MBTA Red Line to Andrew Square Station. The museum is
about a ten-minute walk north along Dorchester Avenue.

The Boston Tea Party, in which colonials protested taxation by
destroying a cargo of imported tea, was a turning point in early
American history. Unfortunately, due to extensive fire damage,
the Boston Tea Party Ship and Museum is undergoing major
renovation at the time of this printing. The planned site will be
approximately twice its current size and will offer exhibits,
video presentations, living-history programs, and memorabilia
that tell the story of the Boston Tea Party. Two additional tall
ships will be added to the current Brig Beaver replica, repre-
senting all ships that took part in the tea party. Onboard, visitors will explore authentically restored ship's decks, crew's
quarters, and cargo holds. The wharf areas will provide additional space for exhibitions, receptions, and displays, including
the only tea chest that can be directly linked to this historic
event. The new museum will also feature restaurants, private
function space, and an improved gift shop. You can give your
input on these improvements and view work in progress on the
museum's Web site.

Boston University Art Gallery

885 Commonwealth Avenue
Boston, MA 02215
617-353-3329
www.bu.edu/art/

Open: The gallery is open only during the academic year, Sept–May;
Tu–F, 10:00 AM–5:00 PM; Sa and Su, 1:00 PM–5:00 PM
Admission: Free
Directions: MBTA Green B Line to Boston University West. The museum
is visible from the trolley stop.

The Boston University Art Gallery (BUAG) is a nonprofit
art gallery featuring four to five annual exhibits curated by university staff or visiting faculty. Maintaining an ongoing exhibition schedule in its current location on Commonwealth
Avenue since 1958, exhibitions focus on international, national,
and regional art developments, chiefly in the twentieth century.
BUAG has a particular commitment to offer a culturally
inclusive view of art, one that expands the boundaries of museum exhibitions. BUAG seeks to present the cultural and historical context of art and to acknowledge the artistic contributions of under-recognized sectors of the population. Each
spring the BUAG season closes with MFA Graphic Design
and Senior Thesis exhibitions by Boston University School of
Visual Arts students. Gallery lectures, panel discussions, and
symposia (often cosponsored with other regional institutions
and university departments) regularly accompany the exhibitions, as do high-quality scholarly catalogs.

Bunker Hill Museum

43 Monument Square
Charlestown, MA 02129
617-242-1843

Open: TBD
Admission: Free
Directions: MBTA Orange Line to Community College.

In 1775, the Battle of Bunker Hill (Breed's Hill, actually, but
that's another story) was fought by a ragtag group of American
colonists. Despite the odds, nearly half the opposing British
forces were killed, causing the Redcoats to rethink their occu-
pation of Boston. It was here that Colonel William Prescott
gave his legendary order "Don't fire until you see the whites of
their eyes."

Scheduled to open in summer 2007, the Bunker Hill Museum
will interpret this definitive struggle through dioramas and multimedia exhibits. The museum supplements the Bunker Hill
Monument, a 221-foot granite obelisk marking the historic site.
Visitors can climb the monument's steep stairs for a panoramic
waterfront view or simply view the museum exhibits and
admire the monument from afar. For ongoing updates, visit the
National Park Service's Bunker Hill Web page at
www.nps.gov/archive/bost/Bunker_Hill.htm.

Charles River Museum of Industry

154 Moody Street
Waltham, MA 02453
781-893-5410
www.crmi.org

Open: Th–Sa, 10:00 AM–5:00 PM
Admission: Adults, $5.00; Students and Senior Citizens, $3.00;
Children under 6, Free
Directions: The CRMI is a short walk from the Waltham station stop on
the MBTA Commuter Rail from North Station. Call the museum for
directions.

In 1813, Waltham was a sleepy farm town nearly a day's drive
from Boston. But when Francis Cabot Lowell and Paul
Moody sought a place to build the first power looms in the
Americas, Waltham's twelve-foot natural waterfall made the
village a clear choice. The resulting Boston Manufacturing
Company prospered and thrust New England headfirst into
the industrial age. Nearly 150 years later, *Life* magazine pro-
claimed the factory the fourth most important development to
shape America. The Charles River Museum of industry not
only preserves this historic site but also documents many of the
firsts that occurred there (among other things, Boston
Manufacturing Company was the first enterprise of its size to
employ a majority of women). The museum's collections boast
all manner of restored industrial equipment, with concentra-
tions in textile, automotive, and clockmaking artifacts. Other
vintage industrial equipment, including several player pianos
and a machine to manufacture paper bags, is scattered throughout the museum. A variety of special exhibits and presenta-

tions, as well as an onsite library, make each visit to the museum unique. Check the Web site for current happenings.

Highlights:

A working turn-of-the-century machine shop

The Steam Power exhibit

The American Innovation Institute

Commonwealth Museum

220 Morrissey Boulevard
Boston, MA 02125
617-727-9268
www.commonwealthmuseum.org/

Open: M–F, 9:00 AM–5:00 PM; Second and fourth Saturdays of each month, 9:00 AM–3:00 PM; Closed on all major holidays.
Admission: Free
Directions: MBTA Red Line to JFK/UMass station. Free shuttlebus #2 stops at the Archives Building and the JFK Library. The bus runs every twenty minutes from 8:00 AM to 5:30 PM.

Established as a comprehensive museum of Massachusetts history, the Commonwealth Museum protects a swiftly growing collection of Native American and colonial artifacts culled from archaeological digs in the Greater Boston Area. Visitors can examine everyday objects from eras before the United States existed, and the fact that so many of these objects were excavated from trash pits might make you think twice about what you leave for future generations to find. The museum also pays special attention to objects unearthed during the Boston Central Artery Project (better known as "The Big Dig"). Free, guided tours are given every Wednesday at 2:00 PM, and tours for larger groups may be scheduled in advance.

Highlights:

Archaeology of the Central Artery Project: Highway to the Past

The oldest bowling ball in North America

Concord Museum

200 Lexington Road
Concord, MA 01742
978-369-9763
www.concordmuseum.org/

Open: M–Sa, 11:00 AM–4:00 PM and Su, 1:00 PM–4:00 PM
(Jan–Mar); M–Sa, 9:00 AM–5:00 PM and Su, 12:00 PM–5:00 PM
(Apr–Dec); Su, 9:00 AM–5:00 PM (June–Aug); Closed Thanksgiving
Day, Christmas, and Easter; Open Noon–5:00 PM New Year's Day.
Admission: Adults, $8.00; Seniors, $7.00; Children, $5.00
Directions: MBTA Red Line to Porter Square. At Porter, take the
Fitchburg commuter rail to Concord. Exit the station, cross at the inter-
section, and then turn left down Sudbury Road. When the street turns
to Main Street, continue approximately two blocks to Town Green. At
the rotary, bear right on to Lexington Road.

The Concord Museum preserves the remarkable history of this
famous town where the American Revolution began with "the
shot heard 'round the world." Start with the brief introductory
film Exploring Concord in the museum theater. Then, continue to the exhibits, beginning with "Why Concord?", which
ponders the question while tracing the region's history back
10,000 years to the first native American settlements. As
expected, there is a great deal of attention paid to the events of
1775, and authentic artifacts such as Paul Revere's lantern add a
tangible element to oft-repeated history. Not content with one
revolution, the museum also examines the writers and intellec-
tuals of the transcendentalist movement. The museum's cor-
nerstone, the Thoreau Collection, features the desk where the
author wrote Walden and Civil Disobedience.

Highlights:

Henry David Thoreau and Ralph Waldo Emerson collections

Embroidered samplers

The Family Activity Pack (ask for one upon entering)

Cyrus E. Dallin Art Museum

Jefferson Cutter House
One Whittemore Park
Arlington, MA
781-641-0747
www.dallin.org/

Open: Su–M, Noon–4:00 PM; Check Web site for holiday closings.
Admission: Free
Directions: MBTA #77 bus (Arlington Heights) from Harvard Square

The Cyrus E. Dallin Art Museum is a tribute to a truly American artist who began life in Springville, Utah, in 1861. Cyrus Dallin's talent was evident early on, and at age 19 he left for Boston, to study with sculptor T. H. Bartlett. There, he settled into a prolific career crafting commissioned memorials, along with inspiring images of Native Americans and allegorical subjects. Dallin's great obsession, however, was a sculpture of Paul Revere astride his horse. He created seven versions of this piece over fifty-eight years, until he completed the one that now lives in Boston's North End. Along with his *Appeal to the Great Spirit*, which stands in front of the Museum of Fine Arts, this is Dallin's most famous work. The four galleries that comprise the Dallin Museum are filled with examples of the artist's lesser-known work, presented in an intimate fashion. You get a great sense of the scope of Dallin's work, from family portraits to commemorative bronzes, and a feeling for an artist who captured America in classical form.

Highlights:

Paul Revere studies

Native American sculpture

DeCordova Museum and Sculpture Park

51 Sandy Pond Road
Lincoln, MA 01773
781-259-8355
www.decordova.org/

Open: Tu–Su, 10:00 AM–5:00 PM and selected M holidays (see Web site for updates). The sculpture garden is open year-round during daylight hours.

Admission: Adults, $9.00; Senior Citizens, Students, and Children 6–12, $6.00; Children 5 and under, Free

Directions: MBTA Commuter Rail Fitchburg Line to Lincoln. From the station, walk north on Lincoln Road one and one-half miles and turn left at Sandy Pond Road. DeCordova will be one-half mile down the road on your right. By car, take 128 Northbound from Boston. Follow the DeCordova signs to exit 28B, Trapelo Road/Lincoln. You will drive approximately three miles to Lincoln center, a five-road intersection. Sandy Pond Road is directly ahead. The DeCordova Museum is approximately one-half mile on your right.

The DeCordova Museum and Sculpture Park is located on the former estate of Julian de Cordova, a successful merchant and president of a glass company. Travel and art were DeCordova's passions, and he amassed a collection of international artifacts that he displayed to friends in his lavish home. Upon his death in 1930, DeCordova left his estate to the town of Lincoln, stipulating that it be kept as a public museum of art. Today, the DeCordova Museum boasts one of the region's foremost collections of modern and contemporary American sculpture in the only permanent public sculpture park in New

England. Close to eighty modern and contemporary works grace the thirty-five-acre site, which makes an excellent stroll, especially in autumn. Inside, contemporary work fills the galleries, with special attention paid to regional art. Enjoy painting, photography, video, and other new media, and then discuss it over a snack at the museum café.

Highlights:

The sculpture park

Contemporary New England artists

Frederick Law Olmsted National Historic Site

99 Warren Street
Brookline, Massachusetts 02445
617-566-1689
www.nps.gov/frla/

Open: F–Su, 10:00 AM–4:30 PM; Call for holiday closings.
Admission: Free
Directions: Take the MBTA Green Line to Kenmore Square. From the station, take the #60 bus to Boylston Street and Sumner Road. Exit and cross to Warren Street. The museum is a ten-minute walk from the station.

After establishing his reputation in New York with work on Central and Prospect Parks, landscape architect Frederick Law Olmsted moved to Brookline. Here he opened the world's first dedicated landscape design practice, called "Fairstead," in 1883. These offices produced Boston's famous "Emerald Necklace" landscapes, including the Back Bay Fens, Arnold Arboretum, and Jamaica Pond, each worth a visit in their own right. A seventeen-minute orientation video entitled From Pencil to Park: Preserving Olmsted Landscapes begins each visit and gives a valuable overview of Olmsted's work and preservation efforts. The museum's first floor features exhibits of a variety of Olmsted landscapes throughout the United States. The displays combine with the historic atmosphere to make a rich presentation, but visitors should be sure to leave time for exploration of the museum grounds, which acted as a small-scale advertisement for Olmsted's business. Guided tours of both interior and exterior (weather permitting) are available on the half hour.

French Library and Cultural Center

53 Marlborough Street
Boston, MA 02116
617-912-0400
www.frenchlib.org

Open: M, Tu, and Th, 10:00 AM–6:00 PM; W, 10:00 AM–8:00 PM; Sa,
10:00 AM–5:00 PM; Closed F and Su, all Massachusetts holidays, Sa
in July, and July 25–Labor Day.
Admission: Free
Directions: MBTA Green line (any inbound train) to Arlington station.
Walk north along Arlington Street toward the Charles River. Turn left
onto the third street, Marlborough Street. The center is at the end of
the block, at the opposite corner on the right.

As the second-largest French language library in the U.S.,
Boston's French Library and Cultural Center has over 25,000
volumes in circulation, perhaps bolstered by it's excellent language course offerings. However, while these features are available only to library members (and well worth the $60 annual fee
if you are fluent), the library galleries are open to the public at
no charge. Exhibits change monthly and generally feature
French artists working in a variety of media. The library often
hosts opening receptions where visitors may meet the artists,
hear lectures, and discuss the work. The center also offers concerts and a weekly film night — check the Web site for scheduled events. Nonmembers are welcome to peruse the library's
books as well, as long as they are not removed from the reading
rooms.

Fuller Craft Museum

455 Oak Street
Brockton, MA 02301
508-588-6000
www.fullercraft.org

Open: Daily, 10:00 AM–5:00 PM; Call for holiday closings.
Admission: Adults, $8.00; Seniors and Students, $5.00; Members and Children under 12, Free
Directions: Not MBTA accessible. Take 93 South to Route 24 and then take exit 18B. Take the third right on to Oak Street.

Just a short distance from the city, the Fuller Craft Museum is New England's only museum of contemporary craft. Modern creations in glass, metal, textile, and less traditional media fill the museum's exhibits. Download the museum's audio tour podcast before visiting for an excellent guide to the latest displays. The museum hosts traveling exhibits as well as those drawn from their collection, which focuses on local artisans. Workshops, lectures, and a nature trail complement the art and allow visitors to get up close and personal with the work. Docent-led tours are also available every Saturday at 2:00 PM or by reservation.

George A. Smith Museum

7 Jason Street
Arlington, MA 02476
781-648-4300
www.arlingtonhistorical.org

Open: Sa and Su, 1:00 PM–5:00 PM, mid-Apr–Oct. Also open on
September 17 for Town Day and by appointment.
Admission: Adults, $3.00; Children, $1.00
Directions: MBTA bus routes 67, 77, 79, 80, 87, or 350 to Arlington
Center. Walk one block west on Massachusetts Avenue to Jason
Street.

The George A. Smith Museum and adjoining Jason Russell
House are home to the Arlington Historical Society and its
collection of local memorabilia. Museum visitors can trace
Arlington history back to the Ice Age, represented by a fos-
silized mammoth tusk. Many visitors will be most fascinated by
colonial-era documents and artifacts, as Arlington was a
hotbed of revolutionary activity. This period is well represented, though the museum is also a great place to explore the
growth of an American city from country village to booming
suburb. Next door, the Jason Russell House has been carefully
preserved inside and out. The eighteenth- and nineteenth-century furnishings reflect the home's long history, but the bullet
holes still visible in the walls harken to the first day of the
Revolutionary War. A particularly bloody battle was fought in
this location, and Jason Russell was bayoneted on his own
doorstep. Today, the house is a peaceful place to discover our
country's early history. The museum also features a bookstore.

Gibson House Museum

137 Beacon Street
Boston, MA 02199
617-267-6338
www.thegibsonhouse.org

Open: W–Su, guided tours at 1:00 PM, 2:00 PM, and 3:00 PM
Admission: Adults, $7.00; Seniors and Students, $5.00; Children,
$2.00
Directions: MBTA Green line to Arlington Station. Exit the station and
walk North along Arlington Street for four blocks (follow the Public
Gardens). Turn left on to Beacon Street.

Still one of the most fashionable neighborhoods in Boston, the
Back Bay was created in the 1860s when developers filled
swampland and built homes with modern amenities like gas
lighting and running water. Initially suspicious, wealthy
Bostonians soon flocked to the area. One such family was the
widow Catherine Hammond Gibson and her son Charles,
who commissioned an elaborate home. Gibson House is still
largely unspoiled, with original kitchen and water closets, as
well as private family quarters. The home is furnished with
family possessions accumulated from the late eighteenth to the
early twentieth century. These include fine art and antiques as
well as everyday objects, which paint a complete picture of
Victorian life for a wealthy family and their domestic help.

Highlights:
Period textiles
Servants' quarters

Harrison Gray Otis House Museum

141 Cambridge Street
Boston, MA 02114
617-227-3956
www.historicnewengland.org

Open: W–Su, 11:00 AM–4:30 PM
Admission: Adults, $8.00 (maximum $24 per family); Historic New
England Members and Boston Residents, Free
Directions: Take any Red Line train or Green Line B, C, or D train to
Park Street. Walk up Park Street toward the State House (you will see
the gold dome). Turn left on Beacon Street, then right on Joy Street. At
the end of Joy Street, take a right onto Cambridge Street. The museum
is located at #141.

Built in 1796, the Otis House Museum preserves the lifestyle
of New England's elite following the American Revolution.
Harrison Gray Otis made his fortune as a developer before
turning to politics. He served as a congressman and, eventually,
mayor of Boston. The Otis Museum is the first of three houses designed for Harrison and his wife Sally by Massachusetts
State house architect Charles Bulfinch. The Otis family developed a reputation for lavish parties, and the house was the per-
fect backdrop for such society events. The Federal-style home
has been restored in careful period detail, with fabrics and furnishings carefully chosen to reflect the standing of the original
owners. The house provides a glimpse into the early American
upper class, as well as the servants they employed.

The Otis home also houses Historic New England's Library
and Archive, see below.

Harvard Museum of Natural History

26 Oxford Street
Cambridge, Massachusetts 02138
617-495-3045
www.hmnh.harvard.edu/

Open: Daily 9:00 AM–5:00 PM; Closed on New Year's Day,
Thanksgiving Day, Christmas Eve, and Christmas Day.
Admission: Adults, $9.00; Senior Citizens and Students with ID, $7.00;
Children under 3, $6.00; MA Residents, Free on Wednesdays, 3:00
PM–5:00 PM (Sept–May) and Sundays 9:00 AM–Noon (year round)
Directions: Take the Red Line to Harvard Square. From the station, take
the stairway that leads to Harvard Yard. Walk into Harvard Yard and
take a left at the statue of John Harvard. Exit the yard and veer slightly
to the right. This will take you to the intersection of Kirkland and
Oxford. Proceed left down Oxford Street to #26 (on your right).

Three museums live under the Harvard Museum of Natural
History umbrella and together they paint a vivid and startlingly
diverse portrait of the species and materials that populate
Earth. The combined museums run a variety of educational
programs for both children and adults, including live animal
presentations, lectures, and seminars. A monthly schedule is
available on the museum's Web site.

Harvard University Herbaria

You will not want to miss the herbaria, a deceptively small
gallery displaying hundreds of glass botanical models created by
a German father-and-son team specifically for the university.
Take time to study these delicate creations; you will find it hard
to believe such lifelike filaments are made of glass.

The Museum of Comparative Zoology

From there, follow the promising camphor smell of mothballs to the Museum of Comparative Zoology. Permanent galleries feature fossil collections (including a forty-two-foot Kronosaurus skeleton), and endangered species alongside rotating exhibits. The real highlight, however, is the Hall of Mammals and its vast collection of taxidermy. Take it in and feel small in the presence of such great diversity.

The Mineralogical and Geological Museum

The Mineralogical and Geological Museum displays a large array of stones and crystals in various forms (you can, for example, compare cut and uncut versions of many stones). Highlights include an impressive collection of meteorites and a 1,600-pound amethyst geode.

Harvard University Art Museums

32 Quincy Street/485 Broadway
Cambridge, MA 02138
617-495-9400
www.artmuseums.harvard.edu

Open: M–Sa, 10:00 AM–5:00 PM; Su, 1:00 PM–5:00 PM; Closed
September 4, October 9, and November 10 and 23.
Admission: Adults, $9.00; Senior Citizens, $7.00; Students with ID,
$6.00; Harvard Students and Affiliates, Museum Members, Cambridge
Public Library Cardholders, and Children under 18, Free; Free for all
individuals after 4:30 PM and on Saturdays before noon
Directions: Take the Red Line to Harvard Square. From the station, take
the stairway that leads to Harvard Yard. Enter Harvard bear right. Cross
through the yard and exit at Quincy Street directly in front of the Fogg
Museum entrance. The Sackler and Busch-Reisinger Museums are to
the left, just across Broadway.

Along with the Straus Center for Conservation, the Center
for the Technical Study of Modern Art, the HUAM
Archives, and the Archaeological Exploration of Sardis, in
Turkey, the three institutions that complete the Harvard Art
Museums have long been the nation's premier training grounds
for museum professionals. This trio of museums offers daily
tours, lectures and classes to the public; please check their Web
site for current offerings.

THE FOGG ART MUSEUM

Around the central indoor Calderwood Courtyard, the Fogg
galleries showcase items from a vast collection of twelfth- and
thirteenth-century Christian paintings, altarpieces, and devo-

tional objects, as well as rotating exhibits. On the second-floor mezzanine, admire post-Renaissance portraiture, nineteenth-century American works, and a small but carefully curated selection of modern masters. The Fogg also houses the Harvard Art Museums gift shop.

THE BUSCH-REISINGER MUSEUM

This museum's small but intriguing collection surrounds the study room, where the public may view items not normally on display by special request Tu–F from 2:00 PM to 4:00 PM. Medieval curiosities sit mere steps from works by Klee and Mondrian—it is hard to imagine a more impressive array of modern design in a smaller space. Highlights include László Moholy-Nagy's *Light Prop for an Electric Stage*, a kinetic sculpture that is operated weekly at 1:45 PM on Wednesdays.

THE ARTHUR M. SACKLER MUSEUM

Upon entering the Sackler museum, walk straight ahead to the special exhibit gallery to see what's on display or veer left up the stairs to the permanent collections. The second floor features the Asian and Islamic collections, with noteworthy fine art, textiles, and ceremonial items. The third-floor galleries showcase additional Asian art, including Indian, Thai, and Cambodian religious statuary and everyday objects, as well as a gallery of Greco-Roman decorative items.

Harvard University Collection of Historical Scientific Instruments

Science Center
1 Oxford Street
Cambridge, MA 02138
617-495-2779
www.fas.harvard.edu/~hsdept/chsi.html

Open: M–F, 11:00 AM–4:00 PM; Closed on university holidays.
Admission: Free
Directions: Take the Red Line to Harvard Square. From the station, take
the stairway that leads to Harvard Yard. Walk into Harvard Yard and
take a left at the statue of John Harvard. Exit the yard and veer slightly
to the right. This will take you to the intersection of Kirkland and
Oxford. The science center is at #1 Oxford Street.

Harvard University has been purchasing scientific instruments
since 1764, and the Collection of Historical Scientific
Instruments was established in 1949 to preserve this equipment.
Now the collection is the third largest of its kind in the entire
world and contains over 20,000 objects dating from about 1400
to the present. Significant instruments, made obsolete by new
technologies, continue to be incorporated. A broad range of
scientific disciplines are represented, including astronomy, navi-
gation, horology, surveying, geology, calculating, physics, biolo-
gy, medicine, psychology, electricity, and communication.
Many objects from the collection are displayed in a permanent
exhibit called "Time, Life, & Matter: Science in Cambridge."
The exhibit is divided into categories ranging from problem-
solving instruments to psychological apparatus, each spanning
several centuries, so you can sense the cultural impact of the

sciences since colonial times. The collection is also well documented in the university archive, adding to its value.

Historic New England Library and Archives

141 Cambridge Street
Boston, MA 02114
617-227-3957 ext. 225 or 226
www.historicnewengland.org

Open: By appointment, W–F, 9:00 AM–4:45 PM
Admission: Adults and Students, $5.00; Historic New England
Members, Free
Directions: Take any Red Line train or Green Line B, C, or D train to
Park Street. Walk up Park Street toward the State House (you will see
the gold dome). Turn left on Beacon Street, then right on Joy Street. At
the end of Joy Street, take a right onto Cambridge Street. The museum
is located at #141.

Historic New England was established in 1910 by William
Sumner Appleton to preserve and protect artifacts of New
England life. The organization maintains many historic houses
across New England in excellent period detail (the Otis House
Museum, covered elsewhere in this guide, actually shares a
street address with the archive). A list of properties and
addresses can be found on the Historic New England Web site
(Gropius House, designed by the Bauhaus architect for which
it is named, is especially fascinating). Here, however, we deal
with the organization's archive, which history buffs will find
particularly appealing. Historic New England's Library and
Archives includes photographs, prints and engravings, architectural drawings, books, manuscripts, and ephemera that docu-
ment New England's history and culture. In all, visitors can
access hundreds of thousands of items that give a detailed look

at local life for the past few centuries. The museum shop offers books as well as reproduction furniture and gift items inspired by the museum's collections.

Highlights:

Ephemera

Jewett family papers

Nineteenth- and twentieth-century photography

Hooper-Lee-Nichols House

159 Brattle Street
Cambridge, MA 02138
617-547-4252
www.cambridgehistory.org/HLN_House/HLN_main.htm

Open: Tours Tu and Th, 2:00 PM and 3:00 PM
Admission: Adults, $5.00; Students and Senior Citizens, $3.00;
Cambridge Historical Society Members, Free
Directions: Take the Red Line to Harvard Square. Exit T-station through
main exit, cross the street, and bear left. You will pass Nini's Corner
newsstand and then the Greenhouse Coffee Shop. Follow as the street
curves right and becomes Brattle Street.

Now headquarters of the Cambridge Historical Society, the
Hooper-Lee-Nichols House is the second oldest home in
Cambridge and harkens to the Tory era. Built between 1685
and 1690, the house has been remodeled at least six times but
has maintained much of the original structure. In fact, it is the
extent and complexity of these renovations that make the
house so unique and give such a rich sense of history. The
house was restored in the 1980s with a grant from the
Massachusetts Historical Commission. The interior is authentically decorated and furnished, in a few cases with items that
belonged to the original owners.

Houghton Library

Harvard Yard/Harvard University
Cambridge, MA 02138
617-495-2440

http://hcl.harvard.edu/libraries/

Open: M and W–F, 9:00 AM–5:00 PM; Tu, 9:00 AM–8:00 PM; Sa,
9:00 AM–1:00 PM; Closed Su.
Admission: Free
Directions: Take the Red Line to Harvard Square and exit into Harvard
Yard. The library is in the Yard facing Quincy Street.

Harvard's Houghton Library specializes in American,
Continental, and English history and literature, and its collection is available for all adult researchers to peruse. Books may
not be removed from the site, but well-appointed reading
rooms are open for visitors' convenience. The library also regularly exhibits highlights from its collection, including manuscripts, personal effects, and illustrations. Such wide-ranging
authors as Copernicus, Emily Dickinson, John Keats, Edward
Lear, Dante, Tennessee Williams, Goethe, Cervantes, and
Lewis Carroll have been featured in past displays. The
Houghton Library is also home to the Harvard Theatre
Collection, which documents the American performing arts.
The collection covers fine art such as theatre, dance, and opera,
as well as more lowbrow forms of entertainment like circuses
and minstrel shows. Scripts, playbills, recordings, and ephemera
paint a lively picture of the entertainment industry over the last
few centuries — a must for any theater or film buff.

The House of the Seven Gables

115 Derby Street
Salem, MA 01970
978-741-4350

Open: Daily, 10:00 AM–5:00 PM (Nov–June); Daily, 10:00 AM–7:00
PM (July–Oct); Open until 11:00 PM on October weekends
Admission: Adults, $12.00; Seniors and AAA Members, $11.00;
Children 5–12, $7.25
Directions: MBTA Commuter Rail or #450/455 bus to Salem. Go up the
steps to street level, cross Bridge Street, and walk down Washington
Street. Go left on Derby Street after the Common.

The House of the Seven Gables campus is actually home to
five historic properties in addition to the Hawthorne novel's
namesake. Together, the Retire Beckett House, the Hooper
Hathaway house, the Phippen House, the Counting House,
and Nathaniel Hawthorne's birthplace create an experience
that feels like walking back in time. The House of the Seven
Gables (aka the Turner-Ingersoll House) itself houses more
than 2,000 historic artifacts, 700 books, and countless photos.
Hawthorne House features displays on the author's traumatic
childhood, fodder for many of his books. Outside, the Seaside
Gardens bloom with period-authentic plants and summertime
café seating. Tours are run continuously throughout the day,
and the informative guides aid architectural and cultural under-
standing. The museum runs special programs for school groups
and the public; check the Web site for details.

Howard Gotlieb Archival Research Center

771 Commonwealth Avenue
Boston, MA 02215
617-353-1309
www.bu.edu/archives/

Open: M–F, 9:00 AM–5:00 PM
Admission: Free
Directions: MBTA Green B Line to Boston University Central. Continue outbound on foot, about half a block. The archive is located in the Mugar Memorial Library on the fifth floor.

Instituted in 1963 as Boston University Special Collections and renamed in 2003 to honor its founder, the Howard Gotlieb Archival Research Center specializes in important twentieth-century manuscripts (though the collection has holdings dating to the sixteenth century). Leaders in the fields of literature, criticism, journalism, drama, music, film, civil rights, diplomacy, and national affairs are represented. While most items can be viewed with proper credentials by appointment only, rotating exhibitions throughout the building showcase pieces culled from the Center's various collections. Expect to see works by major historical figures from presidents to composers to modern screenwriters. It's a rare thrill to see such manuscripts in person, often complete with author's notations in the margins.

Highlights:

Martin Luther King, Jr., collection

Institute of Contemporary Art

100 Northern Avenue
Boston, MA 02210
617-478-3101
www.icaboston.org

Open: Tu and W, 10:00 AM–5:00 PM; Th and F, 10:00 AM–9:00 PM;
Sa and Su, 10:00 AM–5:00 PM; Closed Mondays except Martin Luther
King, Jr., Day, Presidents' Day, Memorial Day, Labor Day, Columbus
Day, and Veterans Day.

Admission: Adults, $12.00; Students and Senior Citizens, $10.00;
Members and Children under 17, Free; Free for everyone after 5:00
PM on Target Free Thursday nights; Free for families on the last
Saturday of each month

Directions: Take the Red Line to South Station. At South Station take
the Silver Line to Courthouse stop. Once above ground, walk down
Seaport Boulevard toward the World Trade Center (away from the city),
turning left onto Northern Avenue at the light.

For seventy years, the Institute of Contemporary Art has displayed progressive, current work by international artists.
Limited space kept the institute from building a large permanent collection until 2000, when they began planning a new
location on the waterfront. In December 2006, a visionary new
ICA opened its doors to rave reviews. Designed by architects
Diller Scofidio + Renfro, the new building is a sweeping
expanse of glass poised at the water's edge. The interior features public performance spaces as well as galleries, which host
modern dance performances, film screenings, and concerts. The
museum's permanent collection is rapidly growing and features
work by Mona Hatoum, Nan Goldin, and other contempo-

rary artists. Of course, traveling exhibits still fill much of the museum, and all are carefully selected to reveal the best and brightest in the art universe. Boston finally has a worthy destination for cutting-edge art, guaranteeing the ICA will continue to grow and expand. Modern technology plays a role in the new ICA as well. Check the museum Web site before visiting to download mp3 guided tours. The site will also feature online art, so check back often.

Highlights:

A growing permanent collection

ICA prizewinners

Isabella Stewart Gardner Museum

280 The Fenway
617-566-1401
www.gardnermuseum.org

Open: Tu–Su, 11:00 AM–5:00 PM; Closed Independence Day,
Thanksgiving, and Christmas.
Admission: Adults, $12.00; Senior Citizens, $10.00; College Students
with ID, $5.00; Children under 18 and anyone named Isabella, Free
Directions: MBTA green line E to or MBTA bus #39 to Museum of Fine
Arts stop. Cross Huntington Avenue (toward the Shell Gas Station) to
Louis Prang Street. Walk down Louis Prang Street for two blocks. The
museum is on the left.

Socialite Isabella Stewart Gardner made it her life's work to
bring world-class art to Boston, and she succeeded perhaps
even beyond her wildest dreams. Her impressive collection of
Dutch, Italian, and American paintings still hang in Fenway
Court, the luxurious space she and her husband (financier Jack
Gardner) built in 1901 for this purpose. The lush settings have
been conserved just as they were when painter John Singer
Sargent made the museum's Gothic Room his studio. Isabella
Stewart Gardner was not a fan of the reigning cold museum
architecture of her time and instead created an atmospheric
setting that feels like a private Victorian home (albeit with the
trappings of a renaissance palace). Admire the great variety of
fine art built around Stewart Gardner's original 2,500-piece
collection, and you will inevitably spy a piece of Isabella herself—be it a scrap of an evening gown or one of ten portraits
by notable artists. The museum also places strong emphasis on
education, and you may view complete course and seminar list-

ings on the Web.

Highlights:

Titian's *Europa*

The Gothic Room and Sargent's *Portrait of Isabella Stewart Gardner*

The garden courtyard

John F. Kennedy Presidential Library and Museum

Columbia Point
Boston, MA 02125
1-866-JFK-1960
www.jfklibrary.org

Open: Su–Sa, 9:00 AM–9:00 PM; Closed Thanksgiving Day, Christmas Day, and New Year's Day.
Admission: Adults, $10.00; Seniors and Students, $8.00; Children 13–17, $7.00; Children 12 and under, Free
Directions: Take any MBTA Red Line train to JFK/UMASS Station. There is a free shuttlebus to the Library every twenty minutes beginning at 8:00 AM and running until museum closing. Take the buses marked JFK.

Situated in a park of nine and a half acres, the I. M. Pei–designed Kennedy Library is a striking monument to one of the most popular presidents in U.S. history. Visitors start with an introductory film full of vintage footage and narration in Kennedy's own voice. From here, a series of exhibits follows Kennedy's political career, beginning with the 1960 Democratic National Convention. The rich displays cover everything from the Cuban missile crisis to the Space Program, all laced with authentic artifacts, period settings, and twenty-five unique multimedia exhibits. There's plenty of space devoted to the iconic Jacqueline Kennedy, as well as the rest of the Kennedy clan. An exhibit on the Attorney General's Office examines Robert Kennedy's role in his brother's administration. Visits end in a stunning 115-foot glass pavilion where visitors can take in a panoramic view of Boston harbor.

Highlights:

Multimedia use of vintage film and audio

The pavilion

The Hemingway Archive (tours by appointment only)

John Fitzgerald Kennedy National Historic Site

83 Beals Street
Brookline, MA 02446
617-566-7937
www.nps.gov/jofi

Open: W–Su, 10:00 AM–4:30 PM; Open May–Sept only.
Admission: Adults, $3.00; Children under 18, Free
Directions: MBTA Green C line to Coolidge Corner. Walk four blocks
north along Harvard Street; turn right on to Beals Street and continue
to #83.

John F. Kennedy's mother donated the house at Beals Street
to the National Parks Service hoping people might "get a better appreciation of the history of this wonderful country." The
recreated environments of the JFK birthplace do just that,
evoking a simpler time with nostalgic artifacts and narration in
Mrs. Kennedy's own voice. Mrs. Kennedy personally assembled and arranged a collection of household furnishings, photographs, and significant mementos. Highlights of the collection
include the bed in which John F. Kennedy was born in his parents' second-floor room, the bassinette that cradled him during
his first nights in the nursery, the silver porringer bearing his
initials, and the piano on which he later took lessons. Guided
tours are available, or you can chose the self-guided audio tour
in one of five available languages.

John Joseph Moakley United States Courthouse

1 Courthouse Way, Suite 1420
Boston, MA 02210
617-261-2440
www.bostoncourthousemanagement.com

Open: M–F, 7:30 AM–5:30 PM; Closed all federal holidays.
Admission: Free
Directions: MBTA Silver line bus from South Station. The courthouse is the first stop.

Named after a well-beloved local congressman, the John Joseph Moakley United States Courthouse was designed with the citizens of Boston in mind. The building occupies prime real estate on Boston's Fan Pier, and the surrounding park creates a broad promenade along the waterfront. The complex was designed to create a friendly public space that invites picnics, strolls, and relaxation, perhaps in stark contrast to the legal battles within. Inside the courthouse, the public is invited to view rotating exhibits with a historical or cultural bent. Displays are scheduled at three-month intervals, and are required to have an educational component (for example, lectures, tours, or interactive elements). Past exhibits have included a history of the Postal Service, a Vietnam retrospective, and work by African American artists, so it makes sense to check the courthouse Web site in advance to see what's in store.

Larz Anderson Auto Museum

Larz Anderson Park
15 Newton Street
Brookline, MA 02445
617-522-6547
www.mot.org

Open: Tu–Su, 10:00 AM–5:00 PM; Closed New Year's Day, Easter
Sunday, Patriot's Day, Memorial Day, Independence Day, Labor Day,
Thanksgiving, and Christmas; Call ahead on Monday holidays.
Admission: Adults, $5.00; Seniors, Students, and Children under 18,
$3.00; Children under 6, Free
Directions: Take the MBTA Green D train to Reservoir and catch the
#51 bus. Ask the driver to stop at Newton Street. Take a left onto
Newton Street. The museum is one-quarter of a mile up on left. (The
#51 bus does not operate on Sundays.)

In his lifetime, Ambassador Larz Anderson amassed an impressive collection of horse-drawn carriages and early automobiles
at his lavish Brookline estate. He shared his love of automobiles with his wife Isabel, and together they purchased at least
thirty-two motorcars. The Andersons left their collection to
the town of Brookline, and the museum was opened in 1948.
Today, the museum has fourteen of the original vehicles on display, including an 1888 Winston runabout. The museum also
features the Dr. Ralph W. Galen vintage bicycle collection.
The museum sponsors various transportation-related events
throughout the year, featuring everything from hot rods to lux-
ury sedans, motorbikes to bicycles, and more. Guided tours of
the estate grounds are led several times a day. An absolute must
for any auto enthusiast.

Longfellow House

105 Brattle Street
Cambridge, MA 02114
617-876-4491
www.nps.gov/long

Open: The Longfellow House is open seasonally during the spring and
summer months. Please check the Web site for specific dates and
times, as they vary year to year. The grounds are open to the public
year round from dawn until dusk.

Admission: Adults, $3.00; Children 15 and under and National Parks
Pass Holders, Free

Directions: MBTA Red Line to Harvard Square. Exit at Church Street
(follow the signs) and continue to the intersection of Church and
Brattle Streets. Turn right onto Brattle and walk for seven to ten minutes. Longfellow House is on the right at #105.

While Cambridge's Longfellow House takes its name from the
famous American poet, he was not the only historic resident of
105 Brattle Street. General George Washington commanded
his army from here during the Siege of Boston (1775–1776), and
in 1791, Apothecary General Andrew Craigie purchased the
house. Henry Wadsworth Longfellow and his family resided
there the longest, though, from 1837 until 1882. They made a
stylish home, full of art and cultural objects from around the
globe. Other prominent literary minds, including Hawthorne,
Dickens, and Emerson, were frequent visitors. Longfellow's
relatives preserved the home and its contents following the
author's death, until the property was donated to the nation in
1962. Today, it is a gorgeous peek into nineteenth-century intellectual life. Collections at Longfellow house include period fur-

niture, textiles, lavish decorative objects, and, naturally, a historic library. The home is so much more than simply a monument to Longfellow. In fact, the breadth and depth of the collections rival that of many larger museums and make for a fascinating and diverse visit.

Highlights:

Longfellow's library

Historic gardens

George Washington's office

Longyear Museum

1125 Boylston Street (route 9)
Chestnut Hill, MA 02467
1-800-277-8943
www.longyear.org

Open: M and W–Sa, 10:00 AM–4:00 PM; Su, 1:00 PM–4:00 PM;
Closed Tu and holidays.
Admission: Free
Directions: MBTA Green line-D train to the Chestnut Hill stop. Walk
south along the path by the chain-link fence to Middlesex Road (you
will see a sign for the museum). Cross Middlesex Road and walk five
minutes down Dunster Road to the museum.

The Longyear Museum is dedicated to the life and work of
Mary Baker Eddy, founder of the Church of Christ, Scientist.
Plagued by lifelong health problems, Eddy found comfort in
the Bible. After a profound healing experience, she devoted her
life to reviving the practice of Christian healing. The museum's
main exhibit, "Mary Baker Eddy: A Spiritual Journey," follows
Eddy's journey from rural upbringing to world religious leader.
Begin your visit with the multimedia presentation in the Cobb
Theater, then delve deeper into Eddy's life with exhibits on her
family, friends, and writings. The Daycroft Library houses 600
volumes relating to Eddy's life and times, including works by
early Christian Scientists. The portrait gallery features paintings
of workers who helped establish the Christian Science movement. Be sure to leave time to explore the museum exterior, as
the grounds are particularly lovely.

Mary Baker Eddy Library

200 Massachusetts Avenue
Boston, MA 02115
1-888-222-3711
www.marybakereddylibrary.org

Open: Tu–Su, 10:00 AM–4:00 PM; Closed M and holidays.
Admission: Adults, $6.00; Seniors (62+), $4.00; Children under 6 and
Library Members, Free; See Web site for group discounts.
Directions: MBTA Green E train to the Prudential stop. Exit via
Huntington Avenue. Cross the street into the Christian Science Plaza
and walk along the reflecting pool. The library is located on the other
side on Mass Avenue.

Since 2002, The Mary Baker Eddy library has celebrated the
life of the woman behind the Christian Science Church. But
while the library adjoins the Christian Science Mother Church
(also worth investigating), it was established as a nonreligious
institution honoring a very progressive woman. Mary Baker
Eddy devoted her life to the study of religion and health, and
became a business and publishing pioneer by way of her spiritual pursuits. The library holds a massive archive of Eddy's
writings and personal artifacts, many of which are displayed in
permanent exhibits. The true focus of the library, however, is
the big questions: Who are we? What is our purpose? How
can we find happiness? The Quest Gallery explores these
themes through static and interactive exhibits, including a series
of computers that allow visitors to add their own ideas. The
Monitor Gallery serves as its counterpart, examining how these
themes are expressed via the renowned Christian Science
Monitor. Visitors can even look down into the Monitor news-

room through a giant window. Nearby, the illuminated fountain in the Hall of Ideas projects life-changing concepts in light. The highlight of the library is the legendary Mapparium: a three-story stained-glass globe built in 1935. Walk through the globe and experiment with its famous acoustics: a whisper can be heard across the dome. The Mapparium presentation, "A World of Ideas," illustrates the ideas that have changed the world with music and LED lights.

Highlights:

The Mapparium

The Hall of Ideas

Christian Science Monitor newsroom

Massachusetts Historical Society

1154 Boylston Street
Boston, MA 02115
617-536-1608
www.masshist.org

Open: M–W and F, 9:00 AM–4:45 PM; Th, 9:00 AM–7:45 PM; Closed weekends and holidays.
Admission: Free. Please note that first-time visitors must fill out a registration form and present photo ID.
Directions: MBTA Green B, C, or D train to Hynes Convention Center. Exit at Massachusetts Avenue and turn left. Take the next right on to Boylston Street and proceed two blocks to the society.

Founded in 1791, the Massachusetts Historical Society is a major research library documenting American history through manuscripts, fine art, and important artifacts. While not a museum in the strictest sense, visitors can view many of these items with proper registration and assistance from library staff. Hardcore history buffs will find the collection well worth the effort: where else can you see the pen Abraham Lincoln used to sign the Emancipation Proclamation or John and Abigail Adams' famous correspondence? Among other treasures housed at MHS are Paul Revere's personal account of his ride and multiple drafts of the Declaration of Independence. A large fine art collection decorates the library, but much of it is viewable by appointment only—call in advance for precious examples of miniature portraits, sculpted busts, and paintings by notable Boston artists. Keep in mind that visitors must follow strict rules to handle such delicate materials. When possible, researchers must use microfilm or facsimile versions of texts. Artifacts and numismatics require a guided tour by the society staff.

Highlights:

Lincoln's pen

Adams family papers

Coolidge Collection of Thomas Jefferson manuscripts

Work by classic Boston painters

Massachusetts State House

24 Beacon Street
Boston, MA 02019
617-727-3676
www.mass.gov/statehouse

Open: M–F, 9:00 AM–5:00 PM; Closed weekends and holidays.
Admission: Free
Directions: Take any Red Line train or Green Line B, C, or D train to
Park Street. Walk up Park Street toward the State House (you will see
the gold dome). You will have to cross Beacon Street to reach the
State House.

It's over 200 years old, but the structure built at 24 Beacon
Street in 1798 is considered the "new" Massachusetts State
House by locals (see also the Old State House listing).
Famous architect Charles Bullfinch designed the state house.
The gold leaf on the dome replaced copper sheathing crafted
by Paul Revere in 1802. The seat of Massachusetts' government, the state house welcomes approximately 9,000 visitors a
year for free tours. The classical interior is full of marble
columns and bronze statues, sweeping staircases, and inlaid
floors. The House of Representatives chamber, paneled in rich
Honduran mahogany, features a series of murals by Albert
Herter called *The Milestones of Freedom*, which depict key
moments in the struggle for U.S. independence. Memorial
Hall, also called the Hall of Flags, is a monument to fallen soldiers. The state house grounds are worth viewing even if you
choose not to go inside. An interactive guide on the state
house Web site helps visitors locate the nine bronzes nestled in
the gardens, each depicting a figure of great historical impor-

tance, from Anne Hutchinson to Daniel Webster.

Highlights:

The Hall of Nurses

The Spanish-American War memorial

The grand staircase

McMullen Museum of Art

Boston College–Devlin Hall 108

140 Commonwealth Avenue

Chestnut Hill, MA 02467

617-552-8100

www.bc.edu/bc_org/avp/cas/artmuseum/

Open: M–F, 11:00 AM–4:00 PM; Sa–Su, Noon–5:00 PM; Closed
September 4, October 9, November 23–24, and December 24–25.
Admission: Free
Directions: MBTA Green Line to the Boston College terminus. Cross to
the other side of Commonwealth Avenue and turn right. Walk up the
hill (west) on Commonwealth Avenue to the main gate.

Begun in the nineteenth century, the McMullen Museum's
permanent collections span the history of art from Europe,
Asia, and the Americas. Specialties include intricately detailed
Gothic and Baroque tapestries and glowing Italian religious
paintings of the sixteenth and seventeenth centuries. You'll
want to spend extra time on the nineteenth- and twentieth-
century American art, however, particularly the many landscapes of untouched native wilderness. The McMullen draws
its curatorial talent from the faculty at Boston College as well
as from institutions around the world, bringing perspective
from a variety of disciplines to each exhibit. All museum events
are open to the public, so check the Web site for opening
receptions, lectures, and films.

MIT List Visual Arts Center

20 Ames Street, Building E15
Cambridge, MA 02139
617-253-4680
http://web.mit.edu/lvac/

Open: Tu–Th plus Sa and Su, Noon–6:00 PM; F, Noon–8:00 PM;
Closed M and holidays.
Admission: Free
Directions: MBTA red line to the Kendall/MIT stop. Follow Main Street
west, turn left on to Ames Street, and then walk one block. The center
will be on your left.

The List Visual Arts Center, located on the campus of MIT,
explores contemporary art in all media. Both well-known and
emerging artists are featured in this space, which was designed
by notable architect I. M. Pei. An artist-in-residence program
allows visiting talent to inspire and conspire with faculty and
students, making for some cutting-edge ideas. The List Visual
Arts Center presents five to eight rotating exhibits annually in
addition to a substantial permanent collection. The center features sculptures by such artists as Henry Moore, Louise
Nevelson, Pablo Picasso, and Alexander Calder and hundreds
of paintings, prints, and photographs. MIT students are per-
mitted to borrow prints and photographs for personal display
through the popular student loan art program. A wide range of
educational programs are offered at the center, including tours,
lectures, film screenings, and the annual Max Wasserman
Forum, a panel of nationally renowned speakers who explore
issues in contemporary art.

MIT Museum–Compton Gallery

Building 10, Room 150
77 Massachusetts Avenue
Cambridge, MA 02139
617-253-4444
http://web.mit.edu/museum/index.html

Open: M–F, 9:30 AM–5:00 PM; Closed during July and Aug. Check
Web site for holiday closings.
Admission: Free
Directions: MBTA Red Line to Kendall Square. Walk down Main Street,
turn left on Windsor Street, and then take the second right onto Front
Street and continue to the main MIT campus. Or take MBTA bus #1 to
Mass Avenue and Front Street.

Right in the middle of the main MIT campus, under the
dome made famous by countless MIT pranks, the MIT
Museum's Compton Gallery features rotating exhibitions dealing with science, architecture, history, and art. Displays are
changed regularly, so stop by whenever you can for an always-
unique perspective on technology and art in the twenty-first
century.

MIT Museum–Hart Nautical Gallery

55 Massachusetts Avenue

Cambridge, MA 02139

617-253-4444

http://web.mit.edu/museum/index.html

Open: Daily, 9:00 AM–8:00 PM

Admission: Free

Directions: MBTA Red Line to Kendall Square. Walk down Main Street, turn left on Windsor Street, and then take the second right onto Front Street and continue to the main MIT campus. Or take MBTA bus #1 to Mass Avenue and Front Street.

Opened in 1922 as part of MIT's Pratt School of Naval Architecture and Marine Engineering, the Hart Nautical Gallery serves as a showcase for the museum's exceptional ship models as well as superb examples of ocean engineering technology developed at MIT. Ongoing exhibits display both recent advances in aquatic technology and classical shipbuilding techniques that have withstood the test of time.

Highlights:

Full-hull ship models (over forty of them!)

MIT Museum (main galleries)

256 Massachusetts Avenue
Cambridge, MA 02139
617-253-4444
http://web.mit.edu/museum/index.html

Open: M–F, 10:00 AM–5:00 PM; Sa–Su, Noon–5:00 PM (July and
Aug); Tu–F, 10:00 AM–5:00 PM; Sa–Su, Noon–5:00 PM (Sept–June).
Check Web site for holiday closings.
Admission: Adults, $5.00; Senior Citizens, Students, and Children
5–18, $2.00; Children under 5, Free; MIT ID Holders and Teachers
with a Massachusetts Teachers Association membership, Free the third
Sunday of each month
Directions: MBTA Red Line to Kendall Square. Walk down Main Street,
turn left on Windsor Street, and then take the second right onto Front
Street and continue to the museum entrance. Or take MBTA bus #1 to
Mass Avenue and Front Street.

The MIT Museum was established to share the creative energy and innovative spirit fostered at the Massachusetts Institute
of Technology, and it's hard not to get excited when you see
what's on display. The museum's galleries present an exciting
array of permanent and rotating exhibits dealing with on science and technology in its many aspects, from robotics to holograms to architecture and design. To visit this museum is to
peek into the future and imagine what's in store. In fact, the
Emerging Technologies Gallery is dedicated to just that — visitors can experience innovation first hand. Artificial intelligence
is a huge area of study at the university, and the ongoing
"Robots and Beyond" exhibit collects automatons dating from
the 1950s to the present. The museum's holography collection

is the largest on Earth, and features some mind-blowing pieces. And be on the lookout for artifacts of famous MIT pranks. These "hacks" have become an annual tradition, and the university often displays memorabilia from them. The MIT Museum also maintains two satellite galleries elsewhere on campus, which are treated separately in this book: The Hart Nautical Gallery and the Compton Gallery.

Highlights:

MIT student "hacks"

Arthur Ganson's kinetic sculptures

Electronic strobe photography by Harold Edgerton

The artificial intelligence exhibit

Museum of Afro-American History

46 Joy Street
Boston, MA 02019
617-695-9990
www.afroammuseum.org

Open: M–Sa 10:00 AM–4:00 PM; Closed Thanksgiving Day, Christmas Day, and New Year's Day.

Admission: $5.00 suggested donation

Directions: Take any Red Line train or Green Line B, C, or D train to Park Street. Walk up Park Street toward the State House (you will see the gold dome). Turn left on Beacon Street, then right on Joy Street. The museum is located at #46.

The African Meeting House and Abiel Smith School on Beacon Hill were built in 1806 in what once was the heart of Boston's nineteenth-century African American community. Today, they are home to the Museum of Afro-American History, also the final stop on Boston's Black Heritage Trail, which includes fourteen sites bordering Boston Common. As the oldest Black church still standing in the U.S., the African Meeting House was the site of speeches by many renowned Abolitionists, including William Lloyd Garrison and Frederick Douglass. Today, it is open for tours and lectures and may be rented for special events. Next door, the three-story Abiel Smith schoolhouse preserves the African American experience in New England during the nineteenth century. Artifacts on display include a first-edition of poems by Phillis Wheatley, America's first slave poet. Multimedia exhibits and a short film describe the slave trade and Boston's place in African American history, while traveling exhibits on subjects from the

Abolitionist movement to African American film are brought in to supplement the building's rich history. Be sure to check the museum Web site for up-to-date lecture and event listings.

Museum of the Ancient and Honorable Artillery Company

3 Faneuil Hall Market Place, 4th Floor
Boston, MA 02019
781-227-1638
www.ahacsite.org

Open: M–F, 9:00 AM–3:00 PM; Closed weekends and holidays.
Admission: Free
Directions: Take the MBTA Green Line Government Center. From the exit, turn right and cross City Hall Plaza. Go down the steps and cross the street to Faneuil Hall.

Chartered by Governor John Winthrop of the Massachusetts Bay Colony in 1638, the Ancient and Honorable Artillery Company was one of the first military organizations in the colonies. The first captain commanding the company was Robert Keayne, and upon his death he left the land at the head of State Street to the city, together with money to build an armory. The gift was accepted, and since 1746 the company armory has been the upper floor of Faneuil Hall. On display are uniforms, artifacts, memorabilia, and other relics from all military engagements involving members of the company. Many awards received by this very decorated group of soldiers are also on display, but many visitors will be most fascinated by the collection of vintage weaponry, including some of the oldest specimens in North America. This small museum makes an excellent escape from the noise and crowds of the market below.

Museum of Bad Art

Dedham Community Theater
580 High Street
Dedham, MA 02026
781-444-6757
www.museumofbadart.org

Admission: Free
Open: M–F, 2:00 PM–10:00 PM; Sa, Su, and holidays, 1:00 PM–10:00 PM
Directions: Take the MBTA Orange Line to Forest Hills, then the Dedham Mall bus to the end of the line (the mall). The museum is in Dedham Center, a five-minute walk from the mall along the VFW Parkway.

It's not your typical museum, that's for sure. It's in the basement of a movie theater, for one, nestled beside the lavatories. And the work is the opposite of what you'd expect to see in a standard fine art collection: Clumsy portraits of humble subjects and lurid landscapes with no regard for perspective. The Museum of Bad Art celebrates some of the worst creative endeavors ever committed to canvas, and does so with gleeful authority. What started in 1993 as one man's quest to rescue bad art from the trash soon outgrew his home gallery and relocated to the suburban Boston cinema. The collection now consists of 250 pieces, of which twenty-five at a time are exhibited. Plan to catch a film on the upstairs screens and leave extra time to take in the art. If you like what you see, the entire collection is viewable online.

Museum of Dirt

36 Drydock Avenue
Boston, MA 02210
617-585-7000

Open: By appointment only
Admission: Free
Directions: MBTA Green Line to Government Center.

Not a traditional museum by a long shot, the Museum of Dirt
is the private collection of Glenn Johanson, who brought home
a vial of dirt from Las Vegas as a novel souvenir. An online
museum (since retired) spread the word, and Johanson's collection grew as samples arrived from around the world. Non-dirt
items occasionally made the cut, as evidenced by Dave Barry's
pocket lint. There is even a selection of rejection letters from
celebrities who denied Johanson a sample. The museum is
located in the Learning and Digital Media Offices of Jack
Morton Worldwide, and hours vary, so call to make and
appointment. It's a fun intermission from all the serious Boston
historical sites and art museums.

Museum of the National Center for Afro-American Artists

300 Walnut Avenue
Boston, MA 02119
617-442-8614
www.ncaaa.org

Open: Tu–Su, 1:00 PM–5:00 PM; Closed M and holidays.
Admission: Adults, $4.00; Seniors and Students, $3.00
Directions: Take the MBTA Orange Line Ruggles Station. From there, catch the #22 bus to Walnut Avenue at Seaver Street. Continue along Walnut Avenue for three blocks. The museum will be on your right.

The National Center for Afro-American Artists was founded in 1968 by Dr. Elma Lewis to preserve and foster Afro-American art through education. Its museum features fine art by Black artists worldwide, including painting, sculpture, graphics, photography, and decorative arts. Pieces come from regions as diverse as the Caribbean, Latin America, and the African continent, but the bulk of the museum's collection comes from New England artists. The NCAAA Museum also features the word's only fully accurate recreation of a Nubian burial chamber. Modeled after the tomb of King Aspelta, who ruled from 600 to 580 BC, the exhibit contains dozens of 2,600-year-old objects. Some are artifacts from Aspelta's tomb, while others belonged to his contemporaries. It's an exciting look at an ancient culture that sill inspires art today.

Highlights:

John Wilson's *Eternal Presence*

The works of New England artists

National Heritage Museum

33 Marrett Road
Lexington, MA 02421
781-861-6559
www.nationalheritagemuseum.org

Open: M–Sa, 10:00 AM–5:00 PM; Su, Noon–5:00 PM
Admission: Free
Directions: Take the MBTA Red Line to Alewife Station. Change to bus
#62 or #76 to the museum. The museum is located at the intersection
of Massachusetts Avenue (Route 4) and Route 2A West (Marrett Road).
There is no public transportation on Sundays or holidays.

Founded and run by Freemasons, the National Heritage
Museum covers nearly every aspect of American history and
culture, infused with a spirit of adventure. Frequently changing
exhibits have featured World War I posters, Frank Lloyd
Wright designs, and antique lunchboxes. You truly never know
what you're going to find. "To Build and Sustain: Freemasons
in the American Community" presents the long history of
Freemasonry in an engaging manner, using a mock village.
Other permanent exhibits honor Massachusetts craftsmanship,
the clocks of George McFadden and, and of course,
Lexington's role in the American Revolution. The Courtyard
Café offers lunch, high tea, and Sunday brunch.

Highlights:
Masonic and Fraternal regalia
Lexington Alarm'd

New England Historic Genealogical Society

101 Newbury Street
Boston, MA 02116
617-536-5740
www.newenglandancestors.org

Open: Tu and Th–Sa, 9:00 AM–5:00 PM; W, 9:00 AM–9:00 PM;
Closed Su, M, and holidays.
Admission: $15.00 per day research fee for all but Researcher-level
Society Members.
Directions: Take the MBTA Green Line to Copley Station. When you exit
the station, you will be at the intersection of Boylston and Dartmouth
Streets. Make a left on Boylston Street and walk one block to
Clarendon Street. Cross Clarendon, then make another left and walk
one block to Newbury Street. Cross Newbury; NEHGS is three doors
past Clarendon at #99-101 Newbury Street (entrance at 99).

The New England Historic Genealogical Society, founded in
1845, is the country's oldest genealogical organization. Their
research library holdings exceed 200,000 items, including
books, periodicals, and microfilm. Over one million manuscripts complete this vast collection, forming an incomparable
genealogical resource. While many investigate their family history at the library, there is much else to be seen. In particular,
the R. Stanton Avery Special Collections feature texts from
the thirteenth century on, from photos and artwork to town
and church records. Download the library user guide and
browse the catalogs online before visiting to maximize your
time.

Newton History Museum at the Jackson Homestead

527 Washington Street

Newton, MA 02458

617-796-1450

www.ci.newton.ma.us/jackson/about/index.asp

Open: Tu–F, 11:00 AM–5:00 PM; Sa–Su, Non–5:00 PM; Closed M and major holidays.

Admission: Adults, $5.00; Seniors and Children, $4.00; AAA and WGBH members get two for one, $3.00; Adult Newton Residents, $5.00; Senior and Child Newton Residents, $4.00

Directions: MBTA bus #57 from Kenmore Square to the intersection of Washington Street and Bacon Street. Continue on foot down Washington for several blocks to #527.

Housed in the 1809 Jackson Homestead, the Newton History Museum examines Newton and New England history through permanent and changing exhibits. Visitors can learn about the areas earliest settlers, immigration to the suburbs, historic post-cards, and photographs, all presented with an eye for local and regional history. "Seeking Freedom in Nineteenth Century America" taps into the abolitionist history of the homestead, which was a documented stop on the Underground Railroad. The exhibit follows the journey of escaped slaves, free African Americans, and abolitionists as they fight to gain and preserve their freedom. The museum houses the Newton Historical Society and holds an extensive library and research collection that may be accessed by appointment.

The Old Manse

269 Monument Street
Concord, MA 01742
978-369-3909

Open: M–Sa, 10:00 AM–5:00 PM (Mid-Apr–Oct); Su and holidays,
Noon–5:00 PM
Admission: Adults, $8.00; Seniors and Students, $7.00; Children
6–12, $5.00; Family Rate (two adults and up to three minors), $25.00
Directions: Not MBTA Accessible. From Concord Center (Monument
Square), take Monument Street north for one-half mile. Entrance and
parking area are on the left.

Built by Ralph Waldo Emerson's father in 1770, the Old
Manse is best known for housing Nathaniel Hawthorne and
his new bride Sophie Peabody from 1842 to 1845. The author's
short story collection, Mosses from an Old Manse, references
the house where it was penned. The home today holds 200
years of family possessions and sits beside a recreation of the
garden Henry David Thoreau planted for the couple as a wed-
ding present. Upstairs, you can still see the love notes to each
other that Nathaniel and Sophie scratched into the window-
panes. The interior guided tour takes about an hour and traces
the history of the homes inhabitants. A self-guided tour of the
property (open dawn until dusk) is free.

Highlights:
Nathaniel Hawthorne's writing desk
William Emerson's clock

Old South Meeting House

310 Washington Street
Boston, MA 02108
617-482-6439
www.oldsouthmeetinghouse.org

Open: Summer (Apr 1–Oct 31): Daily, 9:30 AM–5:00 PM; Winter (Nov 1–March 31): 10:00 AM–4:00 PM; Closed Thanksgiving, Christmas Eve Day, Christmas, and New Year's Day.
Admission: Adults, $5.00; Seniors and Students, $4.00; Children 6–18, $1.00; Children under 6, Free
Directions: MBTA Green Line to Government Center. Exit the station and follow Court Street. Turn right on to Washington Street. The museum is approximately 1 1/2 blocks away.

In 1773, Samuel Adams led a rowdy group of colonists into the Old South Meeting house and plotted the revolt that would become known as the Boston Tea Party. Ever since, the site has hosted spirited debates that have shaped our national policy. A favorite forum for Abolitionists, the Meeting House hosted orators such as poet Phyllis Wheatley when few locations would. The Old South Meeting House has been exactingly preserved and continues to be used as a speaking venue. Today, artifacts and interactive exhibits bring history to life for visitors. A state-of-the-art audio exhibit called "If these Walls Could Talk . . ." tells exciting tales of Revolutionary fervor, mixed with the equally dramatic fight to save the Old South Meeting House from the wrecking ball.

Highlights:
An original vial of Boston Tea Party tea
"Voices of Protest" multimedia exhibit

Old Schwamb Mill Museum

17 Mill Lane
Arlington, MA 02476
781-643-0554
www.oldschwambmill.org/

Open: Tu and Su, 11:00 AM–3:00 PM
Admission: Free
Directions: MBTA bus #62 from Alewife Station (on the Red Line). Ask the driver to stop at St. James Church, then continue up Massachusetts Avenue. Bear right at the fork on to Lowell Street, then take the second right on to Mill Street.

A unique living-history museum, the Old Schwamb Mill Museum is the oldest operating mill in the United States. Established in 1684, it survived redcoat attacks and was eventually converted to a woodworking factory in 1861. Now, the museum provides historical perspective from both a Colonial and Victorian point of view. Visitors can stand on a seventeenth-century millstone and then cross into a office populated with items from the museum collection. Tour the woodworking shop (still producing handmade circular wooden frames in traditional fashion) and speak with skilled craftsmen as they work. You'll appreciate the vision of the six Schwamb brothers, German immigrants who preserved and made profitable this piece of American history.

Orchard House

399 Lexington Road
Concord, MA 01742
978-369-4118
www.louisamayalcott.org/

Open: M–Sa, 10:00 AM–4:30 PM and Su, 1:00 PM–4:30 PM (Apr
1–Oct 31); M–F, 11:00 AM–3:00 PM; Sa, 10:00 AM–4:30 PM; Su,
1:00 PM–4:30 PM (Nov 1–Mar 31); Closed Easter, Thanksgiving Day,
Christmas, and Jan 1–15.
Admission: Adults, $8.00; Seniors and Students, $7.00; Children
6–17, $5.00; $20.00 Family Rate (two adults and four youths)
Directions: Orchard House is a twenty-minute walk from Concord's
MBTA Commuter Rail Station. Call ahead for directions.

Orchard House was the home of Louisa May Alcott from
1858 to 1877, and it was here she penned her famous classic
Little Women. In fact, the novel was largely set in this house,
and visitors familiar with the book will encounter many familiar
rooms and objects. The structure is virtually unaltered since
Alcott's time, when Amos Bronson Alcott joined two smaller
houses together to fit his family. About three-quarters of the
items in the house are authentic Alcott possessions, and they
give a deep sense of the on whom people Louisa based her
characters. Louisa's own room features a writing desk built for
her by her father, a private retreat where she crafted her tales.
A great favorite of Alcott fans, the museum has a bookstore,
chock full of work by, about, and inspired by the author.

Paul Revere House

19 North Square
Boston, MA 02113
617-523-1775
www.paulreverehouse.org

Open: Daily, 9:30 AM–5:15 PM (Apr 15–Oct 31); Daily, 9:30 AM–4:15 PM (Nov 1–Apr 14); Closed Mondays in January, February, and March, plus Easter, Thanksgiving Day, Christmas, and New Year's Day.
Admission: Adults, $3.00; Seniors and Students, $2.50; Children 5–17, $1.00
Directions: MBTA Green or Orange Line to Haymarket. Continue along Blackstone Street, and then turn left on to North Street. The museum is at #19.

Historians still debate exactly how much of Paul Revere's ride actually happened, but the legend holds that he left his home in Boston's North End on April 18, 1775; placed warning lanterns in the tower of the Old North Church; then roused the public with news of British invasion. Revere was, indeed, dispatched to notify Samuel Adams and John Hancock of the approaching enemy, and he was likely sleeping in this North Street structure when the call came. The Revere family owned this home from 1770 to 1800, and it was opened as one of the first U.S. historic house museums in 1908. About 90 percent of the structure is original with the thick beams and ample hearths common to Colonial merchant houses. Artifacts owned by the Revere family decorate two of the restored rooms, and a Colonial garden has been recreated in the home's courtyard. Paul Revere was a notable silversmith, and the house features some of his work, including a 900-pound bell, a small mortar, and a bolt from the USS *Constitution*. A small gift shop offers books, souvenirs, and Revere reproductions.

Peabody Essex Museum

East India Square
Salem, MA 01970
978-745-9500
www.pem.org

Open: Daily, 10:00 AM–5:00 PM; Closed New Year's Day,
Thanksgiving, and Christmas.
Admission: Adults, $13.00; Seniors, $11.00; Students, $9.00; Children
under 16, $6.00; Salem Residents, Free. Admission to "Yin Yu Tang: A
Chinese House" is an additional $4.00 per person.
Directions: MBTA Commuter Rail or #450/455 bus to Salem. Go up the
steps to street level, cross Bridge Street, and walk down Washington
Street. Go left on Essex Street to the end of the pedestrian mall.

Founded in 1799, The Peabody Essex Museum is the oldest
continuously operating museum in the U.S. America's earliest
business entrepreneurs amassed exceptional collections during
their travels, and these formed the museum's core. Today, the
Peabody Essex holds more than two million objects and twen-
ty-four historic homes. The Peabody Essex fine-art collections
are among the finest in the country and cover a broad range of
eras and styles. Asian, American Decorative, and Maritime
arts are particularly well represented in internationally
renowned exhibits. In fact, the museum was the first in the
nation to actively acquire Korean and Native American art.
Children will enjoy the Ideas Studios, where they can experiment with art and nature, and anyone hungry will appreciate
the museum's two cafés.

Highlights:

Maritime collections

Oceanic art

Native American art

Yin Yu Tang, a complete Qing Dynasty house

Peabody Museum of Archaeology and Ethnology

11 Divinity Avenue
Cambridge, Massachusetts 02138
617-496-1027
www.peabody.harvard.edu/

Open: Daily, 9:00 AM–5:00 PM; Closed New Year's Day, Thanksgiving Day, Christmas Eve, and Christmas Day.

Admission: Adults, $9.00; Seniors and Students, $7.00; Children under 3, $6.00; Free to MA Residents Wednesdays, 3:00 PM–5:00 PM (Sept–May) and Sundays, 9:00 AM–Noon (year round). Includes admission to neighboring Harvard Museum of Natural History.

Directions: Take the MBTA Red Line to Harvard Square. From the station, take the stairway that leads to Harvard Yard. Walk into Harvard Yard and take a left at the statue of John Harvard. Exit the yard and veer slightly to the right. This will take you to the intersection of Kirkland and Oxford. Turn left down Oxford Street/Divinity Avenue to #11 (on your right).

One of the world's oldest anthropological museums, The Peabody Museum of Archaeology and Ethnology celebrates the indigenous cultures of the Americas, Oceania, Asia, and Africa. Three floors of galleries display rotating exhibits culled from the museum's extensive collections. Enter the museum directly from the adjoining Harvard Museum of Natural History and find yourself surrounded by Meso and South American artifacts. Enjoy culture surfing as Peruvian ceramics blend into plaster casts of Mayan stonework, which blend into vibrant contemporary Day of the Dead displays. Don't miss the Oceanic collection on the fourth-floor mezzanine, with its impressive array of everyday and ceremonial objects from the pacific islands. Downstairs on the first floor (there are no galleries on the second floor), the Hall of the North American Indian offers a glimpse into indigenous tribal culture before, during, and after the arrival of westerners. A schedule of events and lectures, as well as museum archives, are available on the museum's Web site.

Perkins School for the Blind History Museum

175 North Beacon Street
Watertown, MA 02472
617-924-3434
www.perkins.org/museum

Open: Tu and Th, 2:00 PM–4:00 PM; Call for holiday closings.
Admission: Free
Directions: Take MBTA bus #70 from Harvard Square to the Arsenal
stop at Beacon Park. From the bus stop, walk across Beacon Park to
North Beacon Street. You will be facing the Perkins School for the
Blind campus. The museum is in the Howe Building.

The Perkins School for the Blind History Museum examines
education for the blind and deaf/blind over the school's 175-
year history. As the first school for the blind in the United
States, Perkins pioneered many educational techniques sill used
today. The museum illustrates these contributions to tactile
education, which teaches the blind to see the world with the
fingers. Perkins' first director, Samuel Gridley Howe, devised
his own system of tactile reading and writing, and later invent-
ed the Perkins Brailler, still the gold standard in writing imple-
ments for the blind. The museum has an impressive collection
of machines for producing raised type, some made prior to
Braille's acceptance as the global standard. An edition of
Charles Dickens' *The Old Curiosity Shop* in Boston Line Type
dates to 1868, when the author himself paid for the printing
while visiting America. Tactile methods for teaching math, science, and geography are also on display, particularly maps made
of stitched fabric or carved wood. An exhibit relating to Helen

Keller, Anne Sullivan, and Laura Bridgman features belongings of these famous Perkins grads, as well as personal letters and photos. All exhibits are labeled in Braille and printed text and have at least one tactile element.

Highlights:

Famous student memorabilia

Giant tactile globe from 1832

Photographic Resource Center at Boston University

832 Commonwealth Avenue
Boston, Massachusetts 02215
617-975-0600
www.bu.edu/prc

Open: Tu–W and F, 10:00 AM–6:00 PM; Th, 10:00 AM–8:00 PM;
Sa–Su, Noon–5:00 PM; Closed M and holidays.
Admission: Adults, Seniors, and Students, $3.00; Members, Children
under 18, and School Groups, Free
Directions: Take the MBTA Green B Line to BU West. The museum is
on the eastbound side of the street.

Boston University's Photographic Research Center hosts six to
eight exhibits yearly, each emphasizing new trends and ideas in
contemporary photography. Drawing from the university's collection, faculty, and students, PRC exhibits showcase the best
uses of emerging technologies in photography, from lighting to
motion graphics. All are carefully arranged around thought-
provoking themes. The PRC has an educational component
that results in seminars and classes throughout the year. An
annual juried exhibition is always a source of exciting new talent, and locals look forward to the yearly autumn auction,
where notable photos can be purchased to benefit the center.
Another popular tradition is the Mother's Day Portrait
Extravaganza, where elite local artists photograph families at
reduced price. The center's Aaron Suskind Library is another
educational treasure, offering free access to over 4,000 photography books and eighty industry periodicals.

Pioneer Telephone Museum

Verizon Building
185 Franklin Street #1602
Boston, MA 02110
617-743-9800

Open: Weekdays, 9:00 AM–5:00 PM
Admission: Free
Directions: MBTA Green Line to Government Center.

The invention of the telephone was a pivotal moment in world history, and many forget that it happened in Boston. In fact, it was here that Alexander Graham Bell made his pioneering call to his assistant, delivering the message "Mr. Watson, come here, I want you." The building still stands near City Hall and now holds Verizon's Boston headquarters and the little-known Pioneer Telephone Museum. The Pioneer Telephone Museum features a detailed replica of Bell's laboratory at the time of his historic discovery, complete with a extensive collection of vintage telephone paraphernalia. From early nineteenth-century models to phones that look more like modern art, visitors will enjoy this small but fascinating display that reminds us how many innovations came to light in the Hub.

Quincy Historical Society

8 Adams Street
Quincy, MA 02169
617-773-1144

Open: M–F, 9:00 AM–4:00 PM; Call for weekend and holiday hours.
Admission: Free
Directions: MBTA Red Line to Quincy Center. Walk 1/2 block north along Adams Street.

The Quincy Historical Society tells the story of this important community with exhibits culled from its large collection of artifacts, paintings, manuscripts, and photographs. Quincy was the birthplace of many great patriots, including John Adams, John Quincy Adams, and John Hancock, and the museum pays homage to each. Less famous but no less fascinating are the stories of the local maritime and stonemason industries, each of which shaped the history of our nation. Special exhibits in the museum's two main galleries focus on different phases of Quincy history and the specific accomplishments of residents such as artist Ruth Gordon and educational reformer Francis Parker. Visitors may also browse an extensive collection of rare books and historic manuscripts in the society library.

Roger Ward Babson Museum

Babson College
Babson Park
Waltham, MA 02454
781-239-4570
www.babson.edu/archives/museums_collections

Open: M–F, 8:00 AM–4:00 PM (academic year); M–F, 7:30 AM–4:30 PM (summer)

Admission: Free

Directions: Not MBTA accessible. From Route 9 West take the Cedar Street exit. Turn right on to Cedar Street, then left on to Hunnewell Street. In less than a mile, turn right on to Forest Street. Babson Park will be on your right.

As one of the premier business schools on the East Coast, Babson College has an outstanding reputation for training the CEOs of tomorrow. The Roger Ward Babson Museum examines how the college founder's upbringing influenced his business practices and personal philosophy. The collection follows Babson's childhood bout of tuberculosis, the tragic drowning death of his sister, and his career as an investment banker and president of the Babson Statistical Organization. The Babsons figured prominently in New England history, and a genealogical exhibit traces the family back to the *Mayflower*. The Grace K. Babson Collection of Sir Isaac Newton memorabilia includes a library of over 1,000 volumes of Newton's works (many of which are autographed and annotated in Newton's hand), manuscripts, engravings, artifacts, and other Newton memorabilia, including a death mask that originally belonged to Thomas Jefferson. It is the largest source of

Newton materials in the United States. The most unique items in the collection are the actual fore-parlor of Newton's last London residence and a fourth-generation Newton apple tree growing outside. Also outside is the Babson World Globe, one of the largest free standing globes on earth. At twenty-eight feet in diameter and weighing in at twenty-five tons, the globe is capable of revolving on its base and spinning on its axis.

Rose Art Museum

Brandeis University
415 South Street
Waltham, MA 02454
617-975-0600
www.bu.edu/prc

Open: Tu–Su, Noon–5:00 PM; Closed M and holidays.
Admission: Adults, $3.00; Members, Children under 12, and Brandeis
Students, Free
Directions: MBTA Green line to Riverside Station (D-line); taxis are
available for the three-mile ride to Brandeis.

Founded in 1961, the Rose Museum at Brandeis University is
still one of the premier collections of contemporary art in New
England. Throughout the year, the Rose organizes temporary
exhibitions and collection displays that present a range of modern art by famous and emerging artists. The permanent collection of about 8,000 pieces is internationally recognized for its
quality and breadth. American art of the 60s and 70s is particularly well represented, with notable work by Jasper Johns, Roy
Lichtenstein, Andy Warhol, and more. Recent acquisitions
include pieces by KiKi Smith, Cindy Sherman, and Matthew
Barney. The Rose may be a bit smaller than the art museums
you're used to, but quality of the collection and intelligence of
the exhibits provide as rich an experience as much larger institutions. The exhibits in their three galleries are frequently
rotated, encouraging repeat visits. Check the Web site calendar
for educational programs, most free with admission.

Salem Witch Museum

Washington Square North

Salem, MA 01970

978-744-1692

www.salemwitchmuseum.com

Open: Daily, 10:00 AM–5:00 PM; Daily, 10:00 AM–7:00 PM in July and Aug

Admission: Adults, $7.50; Senior Citizens, $6.50; Children 6–14, $5.00

Directions: MBTA Commuter Rail or #450/455 bus to Salem. Go up the steps to street level, cross Bridge Street, and walk down Washington Street. Go left on Essex Street then left on Hawthorne Boulevard to the museum.

The Salem Witch Trials of 1692 have been immortalized as one of the more bizarre and superstitious episodes in American history. In the spring of that year, hundreds of local women were accused of witchcraft and subsequently tried, tortured, imprisoned, and often executed. The Salem Witch Museum documents this time of terror with life-sized mannequins, lights, and narration as well as exhibits concerning the history and tolerance of witchcraft. "Witches: Evolving Perceptions" traces the image of the witch throughout time, from Celtic priestess to modern Wiccan, drawing comparisons between the witch trials, McCarthyism, and the AIDS epidemic. It's a thought-provoking addition to a classic Salem attraction.

The Semitic Museum at Harvard University

6 Divinity Avenue

Cambridge, MA 02138

617-495-4631

www.fas.harvard.edu/~semitic/

Open: M–F, 10:00 AM–4:00 PM; Su, 1:00 PM–4:00 PM; Closed Sa, holidays, and the Sundays before Monday holidays.

Admission: Free

Directions: MBTA Red Line to Harvard Square. Exit at Harvard Yard. Cross the yard and turn left at the statue of John Harvard. Exit the yard and veer slightly to the right. This will take you to the intersection of Kirkland and Oxford (Divinity Avenue).

The Semitic Museum at Harvard University houses a fascinating collection of archaeological materials from the Near East. Through authentic artifacts, visitors can explore everyday life in ancient Egypt, Iraq, Israel, Cyprus, and more. The Cesnola Collection of Cypriot pottery and household objects is especially rich and reaches back to the Bronze Age. "The Houses of Ancient Israel: Domestic, Royal, Divine" features recreated dwellings from three classes of Hebrew society. The houses reflect the Israeli social hierarchy f the Iron Age, during the time of David and Solomon. Fans of ancient history or religious studies will especially appreciate this portrayal of Old Testament–era life.

Skywalk Observatory

Prudential Tower
800 Boylston Street
Boston, MA 02199
617-859-0648
www.prudentialcenter.com/play/skywalk.html

Open: Winter (Nov 1–Feb 31): Su–Sa, 10:00 AM–10:00 PM; Summer
(Mar 1–Oct 31): Su–Sa, 10:00 AM–8:00 PM
Admission: Adults, $11.00; Senior Citizens and Students, $9.00;
Children under 12, $7.50
Directions: MBTA Green E line to Prudential, or Green Line B, C, or D
to Hynes Convention Center. You will see the building from the station.
The Skywalk is on the fiftieth floor of the Prudential Tower.

Atop what was once the tallest building in Boston, the
SkyWalk Observatory has become much more than simply a
place to catch a view. The audio tour highlighting the city's top
cultural spots is still the biggest draw here, but for your admission you'll also get a peak into Boston's history as a booming
immigration center. In all the United States, Boston is second
only to Ellis Island as a gateway to America. "Dreams of
Freedom," a multimedia exhibit now housed in the SkyWalk,
celebrates Boston's legacy as a place where so many Americans
first set foot on U.S. soil. Interactive displays allow visitors to
explore 350 years of immigration history, tracing lives from
arrival to acclimation. The process of becoming a U.S. citizen
is highlighted as well, and visitors can test themselves against
actual questions from a U.S. citizenship exam. The SkyWalk
also features an exhibit dedicated to baseball legend Ted
Williams. The display overlooks Fenway Park, where, on a
clear day, you might catch a distant view of a Sox game.

Somerville Museum

1 Westwood Road
Somerville, MA 02143
617-666-9810
www.somervillemuseum.org

Open: Th, 2:00 PM–7:00 PM; F, 2:00 PM–5:00 PM; Su, Noon–5:00 PM; Call for holiday closings.
Admission: Free
Directions: MBTA bus #88 from Davis Square (on the Red Line). Get off at Highland Avenue and Benton Road. Turn Right on Benton and walk three blocks to Westwood Road. The museum is on the corner.

Built in the 1920s to house the growing collection of the Somerville Historical Society, the Somerville Museum's Federal Revival building sits at the heart of its community. Museum exhibits reflect the city's diverse population of 76,000, as well as the community's importance in regional development. The permanent collection of photographs, manuscripts, books, and cultural artifacts numbers are arranged to focus on varying themes: immigration, local history and architecture, and newsworthy events. The Somerville Museum is very involved in community education and frequently collaborates with local public schools to provide hands-on learning. The museum's Community Curatorial Program encourages residents to design and plan their own exhibits, which are mounted with the help of museum experts. It's a unique way to keep Somerville history alive and generates interesting and pertinent displays.

The Sports Museum of New England

TD Banknorth Garden
1 Fleet Center
Boston, MA 02114
617-495-1235
www.sportsmuseum.org

Open: M–Su, 11:00 AM–5:00 PM. Admission is limited to 11:00 AM,
Noon, 1:00 PM, 2:00 PM, and 3:00 PM. Hours subject to change
based on Garden events; check Web site before visiting.
Admission: Adults, $6.00; Seniors and Children 6-17, $4.00; Children
under 6 and Museum Members, Free
Directions: MBTA Green or Orange Line to North Station.

Red Sox, Celtics, Bruins, Patriots—Boston sports legends
come in many flavors, but they all share one special museum.
The Sports Museum of New England is the most comprehensive collection of sports memorabilia from the Northeast U.S.
ever assembled. There is a mind-boggling array of artifacts
here, from pieces of the Old Boston Garden to equipments
used by Bobby Orr, Carl Yastrzemski, and dozens of other
local heroes. Interactive kiosks and sports-related art supplement the collection of memorabilia, and visitors will pick up
some unique facts about hockey, baseball, football, and basketball. Each of these sports has its own dedicated area, with
smaller exhibits concerning rugby, boxing, figure skating, and
more. The Pro Shop has all the team merchandise a heart
could desire, plus some unusual items like pieces of the old
Boston garden parquet floor.

Tufts University Art Gallery

Aidekman Arts Center
40R Talbot Avenue
Medford, MA 02155
617-627-3518
http://ase.tufts.edu/gallery

Open: Tu–Su, 11:00 AM–5:00 PM; Th, 11:00 AM–8:00 PM; Closed M
and university holidays.
Admission: Free
Directions: MBTA Red Line to Davis Square. Take a right from the station on to College Avenue. Circle the Powder House Rotary and turn
left onto Lower Campus Road after the playing fields. The Arts Center
is the first building on your right.

The Tufts University Art Gallery consists of 7,000 square feet
of exhibition space divided into four areas: The Tisch and
Koppleman Galleries, the Remis Sculpture Court, and the
Slater Concourse Gallery. There is also a projection wall where
short video and film works are displayed. Altogether, the galleries host over a dozen new exhibits each year, featuring both
student and faculty work and art from the university's permanent collection. The Tufts collection dates back 150 years to the
school's founding and includes portraits of Charles and Hanna
Tufts plus other historic university artifacts. The 2,000-item
fine-art collection includes paintings, sculptures, print, photographs, and more, spanning the centuries from ancient times to
the modern era. A particularly fine collection of nineteenth-
century paintings features work by John Singer Sargent and
Ralph Albert Blakelock. More current artists such as Helen
Frankenthaler and Andy Warhol are also represented, and their

work is often hung throughout the Tufts campus. The Tufts photographic collection is well known, with noteworthy work by Walker Evans, Marilyn Bridges, and their contemporaries.

Highlights:

Contemporary photography

MFA thesis exhibitions

United States Naval Shipbuilding Museum

Fore River Shipyard

739 Washington Street

Quincy, MA 02169

617-479-7900

www.uss-salem.org

Open: Sa and Su, 10:00 AM–4:00 PM

Admission: Adults and Children 4 and up, $5.00; Children 3 and under, Free

Directions: MBTA Red Braintree Line to Quincy Center. Take the MBTA red line subway Braintree train to Quincy Center. Exit the station toward Hancock Street. Take bus #220, 221, or 222 to the rotary at the foot of the Fore River Bridge. Walk through the parking lot to the USS Salem.

Located aboard the USS *Salem*, the world's only preserved heavy cruiser, the United States Naval Shipbuilding Museum is a tribute to this class of seafaring vessels and the soldiers who sailed them. Various Memorial Rooms on the ship's third deck pay homage to U.S. Navy cruiser sailors, sister ship USS *Newport News*, and shipbuilding models. Uniforms, photos, and other artifacts paint a convincing picture of 1959, the year the *Salem* was decommissioned and put into storage. Many aspects of the ship have been virtually untouched since that time. An exhibit on U.S. Navy SEALs highlights the history and training of this elite military force, including a memorial to fallen local members.

USS *Constitution* Museum

Charlestown Navy Yard, Building 22
Charlestown, MA 02129
617-426-1812
www.ussconstitutionmuseum.org

Open: Daily, 9:00 AM–6:00 PM (Apr 15–Oct 15); Daily 10:00
AM–5:00 PM (Oct 16–Apr 14); Closed Thanksgiving, Christmas, and
New Year's Day.
Admission: Free
Directions: MBTA Green Line to North Station. Exit to Causeway Street
and head north. At the five-way intersection, continue over the
Charlestown Bridge. Take the staircase to Paul Revere Park, go under
the overpass, and follow the street to the end. You will see the Navy
Yard on your right.

The USS *Constitution*, fondly called Old Ironsides after the
poem by Oliver Wendell Holmes, was commissioned in 1797
as one of the U.S. Navy's first ships. After more than two
centuries and several restorations, Old Ironsides is still afloat
and can be toured on weekends (visit www.oldironsides.com
for information). Nearby, The USS *Constitution* Museum preserves and interprets the history of this vessel. The museum
was founded in 1976 so that the ship itself could be cleared of
display cases and restored to active-duty condition. The collection spans 200 years of USS *Constitution* history through artifacts, fine art, and personal mementos of crewmembers. The
Model Shipwright Guild keeps a gallery here as well, full of
incredibly detailed handcrafted models. Museum staff and
Navy crew provide guided tours, sometimes in period costume.
Visitors can also spend time perusing the 2,000 volumes in the

Samuel Eliot Morison Memorial Library (a reference request form must be filled out one week in advance).

Warren Anatomical Museum

Countway Library, 5th floor
10 Shattuck Street
Boston, MA 02115
617-432-6196
www.countway.med.harvard.edu/warren/

Open: Daily, 9:00 AM–5:00 PM; Closed on university holidays; check
Web site for details.
Admission: Free
Directions: MBTA Green E Line to Brigham Circle. The Countway
Library will be visible across the street; enter on Shattuck Street in
back.

Like many physicians of his era, Dr. John Collins Warren
(1778–1856) collected unusual anatomical specimens for research
and educational purposes. Upon his resignation from Harvard
University, the doctor left his collection to the school, and the
Warren Anatomical Museum was established. Today, it is
home to 15,000 items of medical interest, from papier maché
models to preserved organs. Some exhibits might not be for the
squeamish, but visitors are guaranteed to learn something new.
The museum's most well known artifact is probably the
Phineas Gage skull, which came from a man who survived
impalement by crowbar in 1848.

Highlights:
Dr. Oliver Wendell Holmes microscope collection
Phrenological collection of Johann Gaspar Spurzheim
Phineas Gage skull
Inhaler from first ether-assisted operation

Appendix

Ten Essential Museums
Boston Children's Museum
Boston Historical Society and Museum
Boston Museum of Fine Arts
Boston Museum of Science
Harvard Museums of Natural History
Institute of Contemporary Art
Isabella Stewart Gardner Museum
Massachusetts State House
Old South Meeting House
Skywalk Observatory

Only in Boston
Boston Fire Museum
Boston Public Library
Boston Tea Party Ship and Museum
Frederick Law Olmsted National Historical Site
Historic New England
Mary Baker Eddy Museum
Massachusetts Historical Society
New England Sports Museum
Skywalk Observatory
USS *Constitution* Museum

Ten Museums for Children

Blue Hills Trailside Museum

Boston Children's Museum

Boston Museum of Science

Boston Tea Party Ship and Museum

Charles River Museum of Industry

Harvard University Museums of Natural History

Mary Baker Eddy Museum

National Heritage Museum

Orchard House

USS *Constitution* Museum

Ten Museums for Teenagers

DeCordova Museum

Harvard Collection of Historical Scientific Instruments

Institute of Contemporary Art

Larz Anderson Auto Museum

MIT Museum

Museum of Bad Art

Museum of Dirt

New England Sports Museum

Rose Art Museum

Warren Anatomical Museum

Ten Museums–Art & Architecture

Boston Museum of Fine Arts

DeCordova Museum

Harvard University Art Museums

Institute of Contemporary Art

Isabella Stewart Gardner Museum

List Visual Arts Center

McMullen Museum of Art

Museum of the National Center for Afro-American Artists

Peabody Essex Museum

Rose Art Museum

Ten Museums–History

Adams National Historical Park

Bunker Hill Museum

Concord Museum

George A. Smith Museum

Howard Gotlieb Research Center

John F. Kennedy Library and Museum

John Fitzgerald Kennedy National Historic Site

Museum of Afro-American History

National Heritage Museum

Peabody Museum of Archaeology and Ethnology

Ten Museums–Regional Interest

Boston Fire Museum

Boston Historical Society and Museum

George A. Smith Museum

Massachusetts Historical Society

New England Historic Genealogical Society

New England Sports Museum

Newton History Museum at the Jackson Homestead

Quincy Historical Society

Salem Witch Museum

Somerville Museum

Ten Museums–Science & Technology

Blue Hills Trailside Museum

Boston Museum of Science

Charles River Museum of Industry

Harvard Collection of Historical Scientific Instruments

Harvard University Museums of Natural History

MIT Museum

MIT Museum–Hart Nautical Gallery

Pioneer Telephone Museum

Roger Ward Babson Museum

Warren Anatomical Museum

Ten Museums–Religion & Culture

American Jewish Historical Society–Boston
Armenian Library and Museum of America
French Library and Cultural Center
Longyear Museum
Mary Baker Eddy Museum
Museum of Afro-American History
Museum of the National Center for Afro-American Artists
Peabody Museum of Archaeology and Ethnology
Salem Witch Museum
The Semitic Museum at Harvard University

Historic Houses

Adams National Historical Park
Cyrus E. Dallin Art Museum
George A. Smith Museum
Gibson House Museum
Harrison Gray Otis House
Hooper-Lee-Nichols House
John Fitzgerald Kennedy National Historic Site
Larz Anderson Auto Museum
Longfellow House
Newton History Museum at the Jackson Homestead
Paul Revere House
The House of the Seven Gables
The Old Manse

Museums with Free Admission

American Jewish Historical Society–Boston

Boston Architectural College

Boston Athenaeum

Boston Beer Museum

Boston Fire Museum

Boston Public Library

Boston Stock Exchange

Boston University Art Gallery

Commonwealth Museum

Cyrus E. Dallin Art Museum

Frederick Law Olmsted National Historical Site

French Library and Cultural Center

Harvard Collection of Historical Scientific Instruments

Houghton Library

Howard Gotlieb Research Center

John Joseph Moakley United States Courthouse

Longyear Museum

Massachusetts Historical Society

Massachusetts State House

McMullen Museum of Art

MIT List Visual Arts Center

MIT Museum–Compton Gallery

MIT Museum–Hart Nautical Gallery

Museum of Afro-American History

Museum of Bad Art

Museum of the Ancient and Honorable Artillery Company

National Heritage Museum

Old Schwamb Mill Museum

Perkins School for the Blind History Museum

Pioneer Telephone Museum

Quincy Historical Society

Roger Ward Babson Museum

Somerville Museum

The Museum of Dirt

The Semitic Museum at Harvard University

Tufts University Art Gallery

USS *Constitution* Museum

Warren Anatomical Museum

Index of Alternative Museum Names